The Student Phrase Book

Palgrave Study Skills

Business Degree Success
Career Skills
Cite Them Right (8th edn)
Critical Thinking Skills (2nd edn)
e-Learning Skills (2nd edn)
The Exam Skills Handbook (2nd edn)
Great Ways to Learn Anatomy and
    Physiology
How to Begin Studying English
    Literature (3rd edn)
How to Manage Your Distance and
    Open Learning Course
How to Manage Your Postgraduate
    Course
How to Study Foreign Languages
How to Study Linguistics (2nd edn)
How to Use Your Reading in Your
    Essays (2nd edn)
How to Write Better Essays (3rd edn)
How to Write Your Undergraduate
    Dissertation
Improve Your Grammar
Information Skills
The International Student Handbook
IT Skills for Successful Study
The Mature Student's Guide to Writing
    (3rd edn)
The Mature Student's Handbook
The Palgrave Student Planner
Practical Criticism
Presentation Skills for Students (2nd
    edn)

The Principles of Writing in Psychology
Professional Writing (2nd edn)
Researching Online
Skills for Success (2nd edn)
The Student's Guide to Writing (3rd
    edn)
Study Skills Connected
The Study Skills Handbook (3rd edn)
Study Skills for International
    Postgraduates
Study Skills for Speakers of English as a
    Second Language
Studying History (3rd edn)
Studying Law (3rd edn)
Studying Modern Drama (2nd edn)
Studying Psychology (2nd edn)
Teaching Study Skills and Supporting
    Learning
The Undergraduate Research
    Handbook
The Work-Based Learning Student
    Handbook
Work Placements – A Survival Guide for
    Students
Write it Right (2nd edn)
Writing for Engineers (3rd edn)
Writing for Law
Writing for Nursing and Midwifery
    Students (2nd edn)
You2Uni

Pocket Study Skills

14 Days to Exam Success
Blogs, Wikis, Podcasts and More
Brilliant Writing Tips for Students
Completing Your PhD
Doing Research
Getting Critical
Planning Your Essay
Planning Your PhD
Reading and Making Notes
Referencing and Understanding
    Plagiarism
Reflective Writing
Report Writing
Science Study Skills
Studying with Dyslexia
Success in Groupwork
Time Management
Writing for University

Palgrave Research Skills

Authoring a PhD
The Foundations of Research (2nd edn)
The Good Supervisor (2nd edn)
The Postgraduate Research Handbook
    (2nd edn)
Structuring Your Research Thesis

For a complete listing of all our titles
in this area please visit www.palgrave.
com/studyskills

The Student Phrase Book

● ● ● ● ● ●

Vocabulary for Writing at University

Jeanne Godfrey

palgrave
macmillan

First published 2013 by
PALGRAVE MACMILLAN

Palgrave Macmillan in the UK is an imprint of Macmillan Publishers Limited, registered in England, company number 785998, of Houndmills, Basingstoke, Hampshire RG21 6XS.

Palgrave Macmillan in the US is a division of St Martin's Press LLC, 175 Fifth Avenue, New York, NY 10010.

Palgrave Macmillan is the global academic imprint of the above companies and has companies and representatives throughout the world.
Palgrave® and Macmillan® are registered trademarks in the United States, the United Kingdom, Europe and other countries

ISBN: 978-0-230-28933-8

This book is printed on paper suitable for recycling and made from fully managed and sustained forest sources. Logging, pulping and manufacturing processes are expected to conform to the environmental regulations of the country of origin.

A catalogue record for this book is available from the British Library.
A catalog record for this book is available from the Library of Congress.

9   8   7   6   5   4   3   2   1
21   20   19   18   17   16   15   14   13

Printed in China

Contents

Introduction

To write successfully at university you need to communicate your ideas, arguments and research clearly and effectively; using words and phrases imprecisely or incorrectly will lessen both the clarity and the credibility of your work. Below is an extract from the first paragraph of a student essay entitled 'Do prisons work?' Read the extract and ask yourself whether it communicates the student's ideas clearly.

Line	
1	Prisons are government institutions that keep those awaiting trial or convicted of offences outside
2	society. This principal of removing people who harm society is a generally agreed function of
3	prisons, as is the punishment such denial of freedom comprises. People would also agree that
4	prisons should act as a deterrent for reoffending and that they should also aim to rehabilitate offenders.

In fact this extract contains several mistakes, reducing the clarity and overall standard of writing and contributing to the low mark that was awarded for the assignment.

Line	Mistakes
1	*outside* – not quite the right word.
2	*principal* – wrong word; student has confused two similar sounding words.
3	*comprises* – wrong word; student has confused similar but not identical words. *People* – too general (an overgeneralisation).
4	*for* – wrong word to use with *deterrent*.

Below is the improved version of the essay extract, with the corrected or inserted words and phrases highlighted.

Prisons are government institutions that keep those awaiting trial or convicted of offences **segregated from** society. This **principle** of removing people who harm society is a generally agreed function of prisons, as is the punishment such denial of freedom **constitutes**. **Many people** would also agree that this punishment should act as a deterrent **to** reoffending and that prisons should also aim to rehabilitate offenders.

Do you need *The Student Phrase Book*?

If you didn't spot some of the mistakes in version A of the extract or you did but weren't sure how to correct them, then you will find *The Student Phrase Book* helpful. Below are three student sentences (taken from pages 172 and 180). If you find it difficult to find and/or correct the error in each sentence, then again you will find *The Student Phrase Book* of use.

> Smith's study is limiting because the sample size is extremely small.
> The data infers that lack of sunlight increases risk of depression.
> Tanen (2000) established that visual imprinting occurs in infancy but later studies showed that this idea was incorrect.

Using words in a 'nearly but not quite right' way is common in student writing and is usually because of one or more of the following:

- not having a large enough vocabulary to write in a fairly formal style that is also clear and to the point;
- understanding a word when read but not well enough for precise use in writing;
- getting the main word right but making a mistake with the words that come before or after it;
- not writing exactly what you mean (for example, writing 'people' when you really mean 'some people');
- failing to spot mistakes when checking written work.

The Student Phrase Book will help you in all of the above areas. It presents approximately 1,200 mid- to advanced-level words common to most academic disciplines and gives you important information on about half of them, focusing on the most problematic. In each of the 28 sections you will find some words that you know, words that are new to you, and words that lie somewhere in between. Combined with the simpler words you already use (words such as *next*, *finally*, *explain* and *suggest*), this phrase book covers most of the general, non-technical vocabulary you will need to write successfully at university. The sentences in *The Student Phrase Book* have been collected over 24 years of teaching writing to university students, and the vocabulary has been well researched and goes beyond other books and websites on academic vocabulary.

How is *The Student Phrase Book* different from a dictionary or thesaurus?

Unlike a dictionary or a thesaurus, *The Student Phrase Book*:

- presents the words in sentences so that you can immediately see how they are used;
- groups the words into ordered assignment functions so that you can find what you need quickly;
- gives key information for just over half of the words presented, concentrating on the words that most often cause problems;
- gives word definitions that include information on context and connotation (e.g. whether a word is positive or negative);
- explains the differences in meaning and use between commonly confused words;

- tells you which other words are usually or always used with the key word;
- contains brief introductions to some sections, highlighting points on analysing and evaluating evidence and on producing coherent and persuasive arguments;
- gives you real student sentences that contain common mistakes, so that you can practise your own error awareness and avoid making similar mistakes yourself;
- has an index that tells you where you can find a word in both the example sentences and the word information tables.

How should you use *The Student Phrase Book*?

You can use this phrase book in different ways:

- **As a reference guide while you are preparing and writing your assignments**
  Use the section headings to find words and phrases relevant for what you want to do at any point in your assignment. By looking through the sentences and word information you will be able to use words that convey your meaning precisely (perhaps words such as *cogent*, *corroborated*, *infer*, *rigorous* or *succinct*). If you have time, you could also take a look at the sentences at the end of a section to practise spotting and correcting mistakes commonly made by students.
- **To check a word you want to use**
  If you want to use a word you are not sure of,

you can look it up in the index, see how it is used in a sentence, check its precise meaning, see other words with which it is commonly used, and find out about common errors to avoid.

- **To check the meaning of a word or phrase you come across in your reading**
  Again, you can look the word up in the index, find it used in an example sentence and probably also find a definition and other useful information about it.
- **For browsing**
  Browse through *The Student Phrase Book* at any time and in any order to help you improve your word knowledge and your familiarity with writing for university study.

How is *The Student Phrase Book* structured?

The words in this phrase book are divided into 28 sections, according to the functions for which they are often used (note that many of the words can be used for more than one function). Each section is divided into three parts:

Part one of each section presents words and phrases within sentences taken from good academic writing. The key words or phrases are underlined, with gaps in the underlining indicating separate word groups. Words with similar meanings are separated by / and words that have different meanings are separated by //.

For example:

The <u>paradox</u> of high intake of saturated fat but low rate of heart disease has been linked to wine consumption.	*Key word or phrase*
Migration <u>is emerging as</u> <u>a key aspect of</u> globalisation	*Word groups that can be used separately, e.g. 'China <u>is emerging as</u> a major economy' or 'The Internet is now <u>a key aspect of</u> education.'*
Creationism <u>is predicated on</u> / <u>is based on</u> the belief that only an intelligent force can explain the complexity of life.	*(/) Words that have the same meaning and so are interchangeable*
Plants have several <u>defining</u> <u>external // internal characteristics</u>, namely …	*(//) Words that have different meanings but that can be used for the same function and in the same sentence pattern.*

Part two of each section gives you important information about some of the words presented in part one. The word information entries use abbreviations to indicate word class, and symbols to indicate the type of information being given:

Word class* abbreviations	Information symbols
n = Noun adj = Adjective v = Verb adv = Adverb conj = Conjunction det = Determiner * If a root word has several different word classes, only the main and most useful ones are given. See Appendix, page 202 for an explanation of word class.	= = Definition* 𝒢𝓇 = Important grammatical point 𝒫 = Other words that are always or often used with the key word ≠ = Commonly confused word/s ✳ = Other point/s to note * If a word has several different meanings, only the main and most useful definitions are given.

Below is an example of a word entry from page 33 to show you how these abbreviations and symbols are used.

---

underlying adj
underlie n

= Something hidden and/or existing below the surface. Often used to refer to hidden causes of a surface action, event or belief.

𝒫 An underlying **assumption** // **belief** // **idea** // **concept** // **principle** // **cause** // **motive** // **reason**.

≠ *Underlie* and *underpin*
These words are not usually interchangeable.
Something that *underlies* can be major or minor, positive or negative, valid or invalid.
Something that *underpins* is an essential, supporting element.
E.g. Government policy is needed to underpin the growth of Irish exports.
For *undermine*, see section 12, page 78.

The third part of each section gives ten incorrect and corrected student sentences that use words from part one of that section. You can just compare the two versions or try to correct the sentences in the left-hand column before looking at the correct versions. Below is a pair of sentences taken from page 103.

Incorrect	Correct
The report emphasised that a desire for results should not <u>preside</u> over accuracy.	The report emphasised that a desire for results should not <u>take precedence over</u> accuracy.

A final point to make about the vocabulary sections is that British spellings are used throughout (e.g. *colour, behaviour, centre* and *analyse*). For *organise, realise* and *recognise* I have used *–ise* but note that both *–ise* and *–ize* forms are acceptable British spellings of these words.

Summary

At university you need to express your own ideas and arguments clearly and precisely, developing you own style and 'written voice' as you progress on your course. This is not an easy thing to do – everyone, from new students to professional writers, struggles with expressing themselves clearly in their writing. *The Student Phrase Book* is an accessible 'way in' to writing at university and will help you to develop your word knowledge and your confidence in producing your own successful written work.

Introducing, defining and classifying

● ● ● ● ● ●

1   Introducing your topic

The first few lines of your introduction should briefly tell your reader why your topic is important and interesting. Be careful, however, not to start discussing your question or issue in detail – leave that until the main body of your assignment.

If you are doing higher level undergraduate or postgraduate work, you may also want to say that your research question is important partly because of the lack of existing research on the issue.

1.1   Words in action

Introducing your topic and establishing its importance

▸ Multimedia communication is <u>a crucial / a vital / an essential / a fundamental</u> part of many organisations.
▸ Ethical <u>issues</u> <u>are // have become // are becoming</u> <u>central to</u> documentary filmmaking.
▸ International migration <u>has emerged as // is emerging as</u> <u>an important aspect of</u> globalisation.
▸ <u>A main consideration in</u> government housing policy <u>is</u> neighbourhood dynamics.
▸ Obesity is now <u>one of the leading causes of // the leading cause of</u> preventable deaths in the US.
▸ Anti-viral drugs are now <u>the most widely used</u> therapeutic medicines.
▸ The study of cosmic reionisation <u>has acquired / gained</u> <u>significance</u> over the last few years.
▸ <u>Recent</u> medical advances <u>have heightened (public) interest in</u> human cloning.
▸ <u>The fact that</u> education <u>is a key factor in / plays a key role in</u> economic recovery <u>is often // is sometimes overlooked</u>.
▸ The <u>concept of / idea of</u> renewable energy is not as recent as is often thought.
▸ Blogs are relatively recent <u>phenomena</u>. / Blogging is a relatively recent <u>phenomenon.</u>
▸ <u>Recent developments in</u> 'invisible technology' have made its use in daily life more feasible.

Emphasising debate and controversy in relation to your topic

‣ One of the most <u>widely publicised</u> <u>debates in</u> UK Higher Education is the level of student fees.
‣ There is <u>widespread debate</u> <u>about / on</u> the potential benefits of ID cards.
‣ <u>Recent</u> medical advances <u>have increased</u> <u>people's fears about //</u> <u>the amount of //</u> <u>the level of</u> <u>debate on</u> human cloning.
‣ <u>The question of whether to</u> legalise all drugs <u>is regularly debated</u> in the media.
‣ The <u>main // most important / most significant //</u> <u>most interesting</u> political <u>issue //</u> <u>question</u> is election reform.
‣ <u>Issues around</u> intellectual property and open source software <u>are becoming increasingly</u> <u>important //</u> <u>visible.</u>
‣ <u>The growth of</u> academy schools in the UK <u>is //</u> <u>has been</u> <u>(very)</u> <u>contentious / controversial.</u>
‣ The <u>controversy over</u> global warming <u>has received a great deal of attention</u> in the media.
‣ <u>The question of whether</u> to introduce ID cards <u>is becoming increasingly</u> <u>complex //</u> <u>difficult /</u> <u>problematic.</u>
‣ Banks are finding it <u>increasingly difficult to justify</u> risk-taking practices to their European customers.
‣ Animal experimentation is <u>an</u> (extremely) <u>emotive issue.</u>

Highlighting a lack of research or discussion in relation to your topic

‣ <u>There has so far been little</u> <u>research on //</u> <u>debate about //</u> <u>discussion about //</u> <u>attention given to</u> the issue of ethnicity.
‣ <u>There are insufficient studies on / There is insufficient research on</u> ethnic identity in adolescent girls.
‣ <u>Previous research has //</u> <u>Previous studies have</u> <u>tended to focus on</u> the ethnicity <u>rather than</u> the age of offenders.

1.2   Information to help you use these words correctly

aspect n	=	One part of an idea or situation that has several or many different parts. Often used in social contexts, for example political or family life.
	Gr	Lobbying is an important aspect **of** British politics.
attention n	=	Notice or consideration taken of someone or something.
	ℰ	Cloning **has attracted / received a great deal of //** **little** attention.

concept n	= An abstract idea or plan.
	Gr **The** concept **of** personalised drugs is new to science. Infinity is **a** complex concept **in** mathematics.
controversy n **controversial** adj	= n – Public disagreement or debate in which different people or groups hold opposing views.
	Gr There is a great deal of controversy **surrounding / over** the use of methadone.
crucial adj **crucially** adv	= Something that everything else depends on. Similar to *essential*.
	Gr **In / to + ing.** E.g. Sharing information is crucial **in / to** solv**ing** the problem.
	ℰ A crucial **factor // aspect // component // element // ingredient // issue // question // role**.
debate n / v **debatable** adj **debatably** adv	= n – When people who hold different opinions present their case, usually with the aim of persuading the audience that their view is the correct or best one. A debate often involves a large number of people. adj – Open to challenge and/or debate. Similar to *arguable*. adv – It may be challenged and/or debated. Similar to *arguably*. (See also section 4, page 22, and section 27, page 185.)
	Gr n – There is ongoing debate **over / about / on** pension schemes.
	ℰ A **subject of heated** debate / X **is hotly** debated. **Widespread (public)** debate on X.
	≠ *Debate* and *discuss* A *discussion / to discuss* involves people talking about an issue where the participants hold different or similar positions, and where the aim is usually to reach a level of agreement rather than to win the argument. *Debate* and *argue* Use the noun *debate* to refer to an issue, and the verb *argue* to propose a specific position or viewpoint. E.g. There is much academic debate over whether creative design is a scientific theory. ✓ I will debate that creative design is not a scientific theory. ✗ I will argue that creative design is not a scientific theory. ✓

emotive adj	= Arousing a strong emotional response. Used in the context of controversial issues or topics.
	≠ *Emotive* and *emotional* *Emotive* is used to describe a topic or issue that causes strong feelings. *Emotional* relates to personal feelings about life experiences. E.g. Funerals are usually emotional events.
factor n / v	= n – One of several things that cause or influence something else. v –To include or exclude something as relevant when making a decision.
	Gr v – Age was a key factor **in** the responses to the survey.
	ℰ A(n) **major / important** // **deciding / determining** // **causal** // **contributing** factor.
issue n / v	= n – Something argued about that affects a lot of people. Usually used in a political or social context. v – To give out or to circulate.
phenomenon n	= Something that is interesting, unique or difficult to understand in nature, science or society.
	Gr *Phenomenon* is the singular form. E.g. Social networking **is** a relatively recent phenomen**on**. *Phenomena* is the plural form. E.g. Supernatural phenomen**a are** difficult to define.
widespread adj	= Something specific that exists or happens (e.g. a belief, poverty, disease) over a large area.
	ℰ Widespread **use of** // **support for** // **acceptance of** // **criticism of** // **condemnation of** X. Widespread **concern about** // **assumption that** // **belief that** // **acceptance of** // **rejection of** X.
	* *Widespread* can be used to describe a debate or problem, but not a question or issue. *Wide spread* and *spread wide* are both incorrect.

1.3 Nearly but not quite right

The sentences on the left contain the types of mistakes people make when using words from this section. The correct versions are given on the right.

	Incorrect	Correct
1	Genetically modified organisms and drug development are two key <u>factors</u> in biotechnology.	Genetically modified crops and drug development are two key <u>aspects of / areas in</u> biotechnology.
2	The question of whether to legalise drugs is <u>widespread</u> across EU member states.	The question of whether to legalise drugs is a <u>common</u> one across EU member states.
3	<u>Issues have been raised on</u> the reclassification of cannabis.	<u>Questions have been raised over</u> the reclassification of cannabis.
4	Cloning <u>acquired a very small consideration</u> until the birth of Dolly the sheep.	Cloning <u>received very little consideration / attention</u> until the birth of Dolly the sheep.
5	Recreational drug use continues to be <u>a controversy</u> in the UK.	Recreational drug use continues to be a <u>controversial issue / topic</u> in the UK.
6	The last decade has seen a rapid growth <u>of</u> the biotechnology industry.	The last decade has seen a rapid growth <u>in</u> the biotechnology industry.
7	This type of software program is a recent <u>phenomena</u> in information technology.	This type of software program is a recent <u>phenomenon</u> in information technology.
8	This is a <u>questionable</u> issue.	This is a <u>controversial / contentious / debatable</u> issue.
9	The use of pesticides <u>forms an issue</u> in the local community	The use of pesticides <u>is an issue</u> in the local community.
10	There is a growing <u>concern in</u> immigration in Europe.	There is a growing <u>concern about</u> immigration in Europe.

2 Giving brief definitions

Defining your terms precisely and clearly to your reader is vital. Although using a dictionary definition can be a useful starting point, tutors usually want you to define things in your own words, and doing so will also enable you to explain something in a way that best supports your argument. You may need to give an extended definition that includes examples, a discussion on alternative definitions and ideas about what something is not. Indeed, defining a term can form the content of a whole essay, for example one addressing the title '*What is freedom?'*

An initial definition usually has a *lead-in phrase* and/or **a categorising phrase**.

E.g. An amino acid *is defined as* **an** organic **compound that consists of** an amino and carboxyl group.

Natural selection **is the mechanism by which** the genetic traits of a population are determined.

Note that when defining something you shouldn't use the word *definitive* (meaning 'the best or most authoritative' as in 'Smith's book is the definitive biography of Churchill') unless as a claim that you are going to support.

See also section 3 for other useful words and phrases.

2.1 Words in action

Lead-in phrases

▸ In this report <u>I (will) define</u> economic growth <u>as</u> ...
▸ Elective ventilation <u>is / is defined as / can be defined as / refers to</u> the use of ...
▸ Total quality management <u>describes // is concerned with / deals with</u> ...
▸ <u>The term</u> 'postmodernism' <u>has been applied to / is used to describe // has come to be used as</u> ...
▸ <u>A broad // narrow definition of</u> well-being <u>is</u> ...
▸ The theory of evolution is <u>generally understood / widely understood</u> <u>to mean / to refer to</u> ...
▸ A <u>generally / widely</u> <u>accepted definition of</u> cloning <u>is</u> ...
▸ <u>One definition of</u> elective ventilation <u>is</u> ...
▸ The study of political anthropology <u>is primarily concerned with</u> ...
▸ Gothic architecture <u>was originally associated with / originally meant</u> ... but has now <u>acquired a (slightly // very) different meaning.</u>

Stating your choice of definition explicitly

▸ <u>There are</u> <u>several // various</u> <u>definitions of</u> quality. In this essay <u>I (will) define it as</u> ...
▸ 'Freedom of speech' <u>has been interpreted in various ways.</u> <u>I define it here as</u> ...
▸ 'Function' <u>is an ambiguous</u> term because it is used in so many different contexts. <u>I will define it here as</u> ...
▸ 'Terrorism' <u>is a highly subjective word.</u> <u>I define it here as</u> ...

Lead-in phrases that refer to other people's definitions

▸ <u>In the literature</u> justice <u>is (usually // often) / tends to be</u> <u>defined as</u> …

▸ Kline (2009) <u>defines</u> progress <u>as</u> …

▸ Progress <u>has been defined as</u> … (Kline 2009).

▸ The theory of reasoned action <u>is (usually // often) attributed to</u> Fishbein and Ajzen (1975, 1980).

Defining by describing elements

▸ DNA <u>is composed of / comprises / consists of</u> …

▸ The United Kingdom and Ireland <u>constitute</u> the British Isles.

▸ Curcumin is <u>a</u> major <u>constituent of</u> Turmeric.

Examples of categorising words and phrases

▸ X is <u>a type of</u> Y // <u>a branch of</u> Y // <u>a system of</u> Y // <u>a style of</u> Y // <u>a mode of</u> Y // <u>a model of</u> Y // <u>a category of</u> Y // <u>the study of</u> Y …

▸ X is <u>a process</u> // <u>a phenomenon</u> // <u>an organisation</u> // <u>a mechanism</u> // <u>a substance</u> // <u>a material</u> …

▸ X is <u>a framework</u> // <u>a hierarchy</u> // <u>an infrastructure</u> …

▸ X is <u>a paradigm</u> // <u>a construct</u> // <u>a concept</u> // <u>an approach</u> // <u>a perspective</u> // <u>a school of thought</u> // <u>an ideology</u> …

(For information on these words see section 18, pages 112–14.)

2.2 Information to help you use these words correctly

ambiguous adj **ambiguity** n	=	adj – Something that has more than one meaning and so may be interpreted differently in different contexts.
	≠	*Ambiguous* and *vague* These words are sometimes used interchangeably but they do have different meanings. If something is vague it means that it is imprecise, unclear or indefinite, not that it has more than one possible meaning. For *vague*, see section 25, page 171. *Ambiguous* and *ambivalent* *Ambivalent* is when you feel unsure whether you like or want something. (See also section 19, page 118.)
	✳	*Ambiguity* has more specialised meanings in linguistics, maths and philosophy.

apply v **application** n	= v – (1) To refer or relate to. E.g. The legislation applies to anyone over 65. (2) To use or bring into operation. E.g. The process should be applied when there is a serious accident. (3) To make a formal request. E.g. To apply for a visa. (4) To put a substance onto a surface. E.g. The next step was to apply gold to the surface of each particle.
associate v **association** n	= v – (1) To connect or link in the mind. (2) Of people, to meet with regularly.
attribute v / n	= v – To say who invented, discovered or first used something. E.g. The idea of using the subconscious as a psychoanalytic tool is attributed to Freud. = n – A quality or characteristic. E.g. Stamina is a key physical attribute needed for advanced yoga practices. ✳ The verb is pronounced _attribute_ and the noun is pronounced _attribute_.
broad adj	= (1) General, not detailed. (2) Wide or large.
compose v	= (1) 'Is made up of'. _Compose_ can be used to describe something that has one or more elements, usually in the context of substances and materials. Similar to _consists of_. (2) To create a piece of music. _Gr_ For meaning (1), _compose_ is used with the verb 'to be' and _of._ E.g. Ice **is composed of** frozen water. Steel **is composed of** iron and carbon.
comprise v	= 'Is made up of'. Similar to _is composed of_ and _consists of_ except that _comprise_ is only used when more than one element makes up the whole. E.g. Ice comprises frozen water. ✗ Great Britain comprises England, Scotland and Wales. ✓ _Gr_ Do not use the verb _to be_ or _of_ (although _comprise of_ is a common mistake). E.g. Great Britain is comprised of England, Scotland and Wales. ✗ Great Britain **comprises** England, Scotland and Wales. ✓

consists of v	=	Is made of. Similar to *is composed of* and *comprises*.
	Gr	Used <u>without</u> the verb *to be* but <u>with</u> of. E.g. Great Britain is **consists of** England, Scotland and Wales. ✗ Great Britain **consists of** England, Scotland and Wales. ✓
constituent adj / n	=	n – (1) An element or component within a whole. (2) In politics, a member of a constituency. adj – Being one part of a whole.
constitute v	=	(1) 'Makes up'. Indicates the reverse relationship to *is composed of*, *comprises* and *consists of*. E.g. England, Scotland and Wales constitute Great Britain. (2) Is/are. E.g. Racial abuse constitutes a criminal offence under UK law.
mode n	=	A specific way something is done, is expressed or happens, often when a choice of different methods or types exists.
	🖉	A mode of **production** // **communication** // **interaction** // **expression** // **thought** // **conduct** // **behaviour** // **transport**.
model n / v	=	n – A specific way of doing or behaving, usually seen as a good example or standard.
	🖉	A **basic** // **conventional** / **traditional** // **common** // **dominant** // **standard** // **excellent** // **positive** // **successful** model. A model of **best practice** // **excellence** // **good behaviour**. To **follow** / **adopt** / **use** / **apply** a model.
refer to v	=	*Refer* has several meanings but when used to give a definition it means 'is the word/term used for'. E.g. Scumbling refers to the technique of applying a thin covering of opaque colour to a painting.
	≠	*Refers to* and *relates to* *Relates to* means 'is connected to'. These two phrases are sometimes used interchangeably, but you should use *refers to* when you are defining something.

2.3   Nearly but not quite right

The sentences on the left contain the types of mistakes people make when using words from this section. The correct versions are given on the right.

	Incorrect	Correct
1	'Poverty' is an <u>ambivalent</u> term. I will define it here as …	'Poverty' is an <u>ambiguous</u> term. I will define it here as …
2	A law firm <u>comprises of</u> a group of lawyers working together under a specific name.	A law firm <u>comprises / is composed of / consists of</u> a group of lawyers working together under a specific name.
3	Cognitive therapy <u>is concerning</u> challenging the client's negative core beliefs and thought patterns.	Cognitive therapy <u>concerns / is concerned with</u> challenging the client's negative core beliefs and thought patterns.
4	Many people view the practice of animal testing as <u>consisting of</u> many flaws.	Many people view the practice of animal testing as <u>having</u> many flaws.
5	My essay <u>consists of</u> the similarities and differences between the UK and American legal system.	My essay <u>discusses / analyses / examines</u> … the similarities and differences between the UK and American legal system.
6	Cranial implants are one potential future <u>model</u> of communication.	Cranial implants are one potential future <u>mode</u> of communication.
7	The term 'ethnic group' <u>relates to</u> a group of people who share (or believe they share) a common heritage.	The term 'ethnic group' <u>refers to</u> a group of people who share (or believe they share) a common heritage.
8	The first use of the term 'psychology' is <u>attributed by</u> Gockel.	The first use of the term 'psychology' is <u>attributed to</u> Gockel.
9	An intake of approximately 30% protein, 40% carbohydrate and not more than 30% 'good' fats <u>consists of</u> a healthy diet.	An intake of approximately 30% protein, 40% carbohydrate and not more than 30% 'good' fats <u>constitutes</u> a healthy diet.
10	A <u>wide</u> definition of competitive intelligence is the sharing of information about customers, products and competitors.	A <u>broad</u> definition of competitive intelligence is the sharing of information about customers, products and competitors.

3 Classifying and describing characteristics

This section contains words and phrases to use when giving an extended definition and/or description of something. You will probably also need to use words and phrases from section 2, particularly words such as *consist*, *comprise* and *constituent*. You may also need words for expressing difference (e.g. *distinguish*, *differentiate*, *distinction* and *discrete*), covered in section 21, page 134.

3.1 Words in action

Grouping into categories

▸ There are five <u>categories of / classes of</u> pigment.
▸ Economic models <u>can be classified / can be categorised</u> <u>according to / on the basis of</u> their intended function.
▸ Economic models <u>are classified as</u> discrete or continuous, <u>depending on whether</u> all the variables are quantitative.
▸ The journal deals with medicine and <u>related / allied</u> sciences.
▸ Latin <u>falls into the group of / comes under the category of</u> extinct Italic languages.
▸ The Italic languages form a <u>subgroup within / subgroup of</u> the Indo-European language family.
▸ The Indo-European languages <u>can be further sub-divided into</u> twelve distinct branches.
▸ AO is one of the four blood <u>subtypes</u>.
▸ The students were interviewed in groups according to their <u>respective</u> disciplines.
▸ Education is an important <u>sphere of</u> economic activity in Western societies.
▸ WikiLeaks provides a way of bringing source material into the public <u>domain</u> anonymously.

Using your own categories

▸ I <u>have based my</u> classification on / categorisation on three criteria: weight, cost and size.
▸ <u>I suggest // I have adopted // I have devised</u> a classification / a categorisation <u>based on</u> …
▸ <u>We suggest that</u> our model should be <u>classified as</u> quantitative because …
▸ I <u>classified / categorised</u> each metal <u>according to</u> weight.

Describing uniqueness and specificity

▸ When it first opened, the Body Shop represented a <u>unique</u> management style.
▸ Earth remains <u>the sole</u> example of a life-supporting planet.
▸ Polonium is the <u>exception</u> in group 16 of the periodic table.
▸ The gene is expressed <u>specifically</u> in stromal cells surrounding invasive breast tumours.

Naming the members of a group or giving examples of them

- There are two main subspecies of chimpanzee, <u>namely</u> bonobos and the common chimpanzee.
- Toxic heavy metals used in industrial processes <u>include</u> aluminium and cadmium.
- There are many toxic heavy metals that are used in industrial processes, <u>for example</u> aluminium and cadmium.
- The Gulf Coast Cenozoic sediments <u>are an (excellent) example of / exemplify</u> extracontinental sedimentation.

Emphasising particular members of a group

- Flavonoids, <u>especially / particularly // notably // chiefly / mainly</u> those found in tea, are potent antioxidants.
- Studies have shown that flavonoids are antioxidants. <u>In particular,</u> those found in tea are effective oxidation inhibitors.

Specifying exclusions

- All students, <u>with the exception of / except (for) / apart from</u> those on distance courses, must sit the exam.

Describing overarching categories or systems

- 'Agrochemical' is <u>a generic / an umbrella</u> term for any chemical product used in agriculture.
- The SGC report gives <u>overarching</u> principles that are to be applied when sentencing offenders.
- The previously separate provinces have recently been <u>subsumed under</u> the new national state.
- Numerous safety features are now <u>incorporated</u> as standard.
- The social sciences <u>encompass</u> a wide range of disciplines.

Describing range

- The human body is designed to deal with only <u>a narrow range of</u> blood glucose levels.
- Since the 1950s <u>an extensive /a wide</u> range of research on leadership behaviour has been conducted.
- There is a seemingly <u>infinite range of / variety of / number of</u> wines currently available in supermarkets.
- Both government and voters are increasingly aware that water is a <u>finite</u> resource.

Classifying by emphasising difference (See also section 21, page 134.)

- In traditional theology, the presence of a soul <u>differentiates</u> humans from animals.
- Previous research has <u>distinguished</u> atoms by their state of oxidisation.
- <u>A distinction needs to be made / needs to be drawn between</u> size and volume.

- There are two <u>distinct / discrete</u> categories of Bengali literature.
- The <u>dichotomy / division</u> between conscious and unconscious movement has been challenged in recent studies.

Describing characteristics

- Both theories share two <u>key / fundamental / essential</u> <u>characteristics / traits / features / attributes / qualities</u>.
- Plants have several <u>defining</u> <u>external // internal</u> <u>characteristics</u>, namely …
- For an organism to count as a bacterium it must <u>satisfy / fit / meet / fulfil</u> <u>the criterion of</u> being unicellular.
- Cortisol <u>is referred to as</u> a stress hormone <u>because</u> it is secreted in greater amounts in response to stress.
- A <u>typical</u> characteristic of cluster headaches is that they occur during seasonal change.
- This sub-species of black bear demonstrates several <u>atypical</u> features.
- Strong leaders tend to have certain <u>intrinsic</u> qualities in common.
- In Christian theology, original sin is the <u>inherent / innate</u> state of imperfection with which humans are born.
- Research shows that it is not urinary tract infection <u>per se</u> that causes kidney disease, but other underlying abnormalities.
- <u>Extrinsic</u> motivation comes from external sources such as a reward, coercion or fear of punishment.
- String theory is a highly <u>abstract</u> mathematical model.

3.2   Information to help you use these words correctly

abstract adj / n / v	= adj – Based on ideas or feelings, not physical things.
	= n – A summary at the start of an academic article or report.
	= v – (1) To remove or take something out of something else. Similar to *to extract*. (2) To think about something in a theoretical or abstract way. This use of *to abstract* is not common.
	ℰ adj – An abstract **concept** / **idea** // **theory** // **model** // **principle**.

adopt v **adoption** n	= v – (1) To choose to take or follow a course of action or idea. (2) To become the legal parent of a child and raise it as your own. ⌀ The policy has been **widely // generally** adopted. To adopt a **plan // policy // strategy // practice // principle // position / stance / approach // attitude // method**.
allied adj	= (1) Of a similar type or nature. (2) Joined or closely related. (3) Relating to people engaged in war who have a common cause.
attribute v / n	= n – A quality or characteristic. E.g. Stamina is a key physical attribute needed for advanced yoga practices. v – To say who invented, discovered or first used something. (See also section 2, page 8.) E.g. The idea of using the subconscious as a psychoanalytic tool is attributed to Freud.
basis n	= The underlying foundation or support of a process, action or idea. ⌀ **On the basis of** X // X **has no basis in fact** // X **forms the basis of** Y // **To do** X **on a regular basis**.
categorise v **category** n **categorisation** n	= v – To group elements according to shared characteristics or to put an element into a particular group. Similar to *classify*. Gr Businesses **are** usually categorised **into / according to** three groups. Marx should not **be** categorised **as** simply a socialist.
classify v **class** n **classification** n **classified** adj	= v – To group elements according to shared characteristics or to put an element into a particular group. Similar to *categorise*. ∗ The adjective *classified* has the additional meanings of (1) being officially secret or (2) relating to newspaper advertisements.

criterion n	= (1) A principle or standard by which things are judged or measured. (2) A key characteristic. *Gr* Criter**ion** is the singular form. E.g. The key **criterion** for a fungus **is** that it does not contain chlorophyll. Criter**ia** is the plural form. E.g. There are three key **criteria**.
domain n	= A specific area of activity. Similar to *sphere*. *⌀* The / A **political** // **social** // **public** // **private** // **male** // **female** domain. ≠ *Domain* and *realm* *Realm* has a similar meaning to *domain* and *sphere* but is less common. *Realm* is usually used when talking about knowledge, experience or imagination. E.g. Outside / Within the realms of possibility.
encompass v	= To include a large number or wide range of different things. E.g. Our study encompassed students from all the different disciplines at the institution.
especially adv	= (1) Particularly, or above all. E.g. Childhood traumas, especially those involving death, affect behaviour in adulthood. (2) Very, outstandingly, exceptionally. E.g. The government is especially keen to reduce income tax. The chemical has an especially strong smell. ≠ *Especially* and *specially* *Special* and *specially* have the meaning of unique or 'only for this purpose'. E.g. The designer uses a special design. The software is specially designed for students. If you mean 'only for this purpose' it is clearer to use *specifically* (see below). Confusingly, when speaking, people sometimes use *specially* as an informal form of meaning (1) of *especially*. E.g. 'I get cold easily, (e)specially if I'm tired'.

exception n	= Something that is different in some way from all the other things mentioned. (See also section 9, page 58.)
	∂ A **notable** // **rare** // **odd** // **obvious** exception. The **only** / **sole** exception.
	≠ *Exception* and *exemption* An *exemption* means 'to be freed from a (legal) obligation'.
extrinsic adj	= Coming from outside, or an external element.
	∂ An extrinsic **force** / **influence** / **value** / **motivation** / **reward**.
generic adj	= Non-specific, general.
incorporate v **incorporation** n	= v – To add or include something as part of something else. E.g. After the trial period we decided to incorporate face-to-face interviews into our study.
inherent adj	= Fundamental and/or unavoidable. Similar to *intrinsic*.
	Gr There are risks inherent to this operation (n). There are inherent risks with this operation (n). There are inherent risks in operating (gerund/v)
	∂ (An) inherent **bias** // **ambiguity** // **contradiction** // **flaw** // **limitation** // **tension** // **weakness** // **uncertainty** // **danger** // **risk** // **problem** // **difficulty** // **quality** // **tendency** // **ability** // **strength**.
innate adj	= Natural, something with which you are born. Used to describe the nature and characteristics of things.
	Gr Children seem to have an **innate** knowledge of grammatical structure.
	∂ Innate **talent** // **knowledge** // **behaviour** // **response** // **wisdom**.
	≠ *Inherent*, *intrinsic* and *innate* There is some overlap between all three words. However, *inherent* and *intrinsic* are closer synonyms, with *innate* being used to emphasise inborn, natural qualities.
intrinsic adj	= Fundamental and/or unavoidable. Similar to *inherent*.
	Gr Money has no **intrinsic** value. Beauty is **intrinsic to** art.
	∂ Intrinsic **value** / **worth** // **motivation** // **property** // **function**.

namely adv	=	'That is'. Similar to the abbreviation *i.e.*
	≠	*Namely* and *for example* If you use *namely* you must list <u>all</u> the items in the set or group, not just a few examples.
overarching adj	=	Covering or including all the others. All-encompassing.
particular adj **particularly** adv	=	adj – (1) Denoting an individual member of a group. E.g. We have identified the particular molecule that … (2) Great, to a great degree, worthy of note. E.g. We need to take particular care in how we define morality. (3) (Of people) fussy. E.g. He is very particular about where he sits. adv – (1) Very, especially. E.g. I am particularly interested in how people respond to subliminal advertising. (2) Especially, above all. E.g. Children, particularly those between 10 and 16, are affected by peer pressure.
	✳	*In particular* is used with a different grammatical structure. E.g. Children are affected by peer pressure. In particular, children between 10 and 16 find it hard to resist …
per se n	=	Considered by, of, or in itself.
	✳	*Per se* is often used with an initial concession. E.g. I am not opposed to guns per se but I am against private gun ownership.
respective adj **respectively** adv	=	adj – Different or separate. Used to refer to two or more groups or people. *Respective* emphasises the separateness of the things mentioned. E.g. After the interviews, the management team discussed the respective merits of each candidate. adv – Separately and in the same order as the items just mentioned. E.g. The <u>Fisher-Race</u> and the **Wiener** systems are referred to as <u>CDE</u> and **Rh-Hr** respectively. (See also section 6, page 38.)

sole adj	= The only (one).
	🖉 The sole **exception** // **aim** // **objective** // **purpose** // **cause** // **intention** // **reason** // **justification** // **exception** // **means**. Sole **control** // **authority** // **charge**.
specifically adv **specific** adj **specificity** n	= adv – 'Only for that one (specific) purpose or thing'. E.g. The software program was designed specifically for use by children under ten.
	≠ *Specifically* and *particularly* As shown here and above, these words have different meanings. E.g. The government is particularly keen to reduce tax. = The government is very / especially keen to reduce tax. The report looks specifically at ways of reducing income tax. = The report looks only at ways of reducing tax.
sphere n	= An area of activity, interest or influence. Similar to *domain*.
	🖉 The **private** // **public** // **political** // **social** // **economic** sphere.
subsume v	= When something is put into or absorbed into a larger group, often losing its individual status.
	Gr Often used in the passive form. The small college was subsumed **by / into / within** the university in 1889.
trait n	= A characteristic or quality, usually of a person.
	🖉 A **genetic** / **inherited** // **personality** // **behavioural** trait.
unique adj	= The only one that exists. *Unique* often emphasises that something is special and/or unusual. E.g. A unique **opportunity** // **viewpoint** // **collection** // **situation**.

3.3 Nearly but not quite right

The sentences on the left contain the types of mistakes people make when using words from this section. The correct versions are given on the right.

	Incorrect	Correct
1	It is not always helpful to <u>categorise</u> people <u>into</u> ethnic groups.	It is not always helpful to <u>categorise / classify</u> people <u>by / according to / in terms</u> of ethnic groups.
2	The heavy metals in chemistry <u>encompass</u> plutonium.	The heavy metals in chemistry <u>include</u> plutonium.
3	There is one overriding <u>criteria</u> a defendant must meet before being granted an appeal.	There is one overriding <u>criterion</u> a defendant must meet before being granted an appeal.
4	Fuels can contain heavy metals, <u>specially</u> those derived from waste.	Fuels can contain heavy metals, <u>especially / particularly</u> those derived from waste.
5	Stem cells can grow into any <u>other cell</u> in the body.	Stem cells can grow into any other <u>type of cell / cell type</u> in the body.
6	Aristotle distinguished five different types of democracy but in modern times they are often <u>subsumed into</u> one overarching category.	Aristotle distinguished five different types of democracy but in modern times they are often <u>subsumed under</u> one overarching category.
7	The client claimed there were <u>outside</u> factors which made it difficult to fulfil the contract.	The client claimed there were <u>extrinsic / external</u> factors which made it difficult to fulfil the contract.
8	Most <u>spheres in</u> life involve the need to negotiate in some way with others.	Most <u>spheres of</u> life involve the need to negotiate in some way with others.
9	The classical view of the physical world consisted of five elements, <u>namely</u> Earth and Fire.	The classical view of the physical world consisted of five elements, <u>for example</u> Earth and Fire.
10	This essay will discuss whether there is a valid <u>bases of</u> the belief that poverty causes crime.	This essay will discuss whether there is a valid <u>basis for</u> the belief that poverty causes crime.

Talking about aim and proposition

● ● ● ● ● ●

4   Stating your aim, proposition and scope

This section gives you vocabulary for telling your reader your specific aim – what it is you intend to test, discuss or argue. Your aim might be to investigate and discuss a point before arriving at a final conclusion (e.g. 'I will examine whether community service is effective') or you might make a specific claim of which you try to persuade your reader (e.g. 'I argue that …'). A general term for these different types of statement is 'thesis statement'. If you find it difficult to form your thesis statement, it may be because you are not yet clear about what you want to say. If this is the case, you probably need to go back and do some more thinking and/or research. Remember to keep an open mind as you write your draft paper – it is a normal and positive part of the writing and thinking process to refine or even change your initial viewpoint by the time you come to write the final version.

4.1   Words in action

Stating your aim

▸ The (principal) <u>purpose / objective / aim / goal of</u> this report is to <u>identify</u> solutions to the company's problems.

▸ This report <u>aims // attempts</u> <u>to establish</u> the most likely causes of low job satisfaction.

▸ This study <u>focuses on / centres on / is concerned with</u> <u>the specific causes of</u> relative poverty in the US.

▸ I will <u>outline</u> the criticisms of Maslow's model <u>and then</u> <u>elaborate on / expand on</u> the particular claim that it is ethnocentric.

▸ In this review we will <u>enumerate</u> the mechanisms and implications of somatic cell nuclear transfer.

▸ This report <u>gives a brief overview of</u> current research on nuclear transfer and then <u>discusses</u> problems with this technique.

▸ I give a short <u>descriptive</u> account of the 2008 financial collapse followed by an <u>exploratory</u> discussion of possible causes.

- I will discuss two different <u>aspects of</u> business ethics; as an area of study and as a social practice.
- I will <u>examine / investigate / look at / address</u> the <u>question of / issue of whether</u> computer games are a factor in youth violence.
- This article <u>gives a critical account of</u> current thinking on evolutionary theory.
- In our report we <u>speculate</u> on the extent to which a student's personality determines their final level of award.
- This project <u>analyses</u> the data and <u>offers a tentative explanation</u> for the high rate of elm disease in Southern England.

Making a specific claim

- <u>I will show that</u> there is a causal link between number of siblings and average adult earnings.
- <u>I argue that</u> // <u>I propose that</u> having an ethical approach is a significant factor in the success of a business.
- Wilfred Owen was <u>debatably / arguably</u> the most influential poet of the First World War.
- This essay <u>challenges</u> <u>the view that / the idea that</u> grammar should be taught explicitly in the classroom.
- I will <u>contest / refute the claim that</u> playing violent computer games contributes to violent behaviour.

Stating your scope

- I will discuss cloning <u>within the wider context of</u> genetic research.
- It is (not) <u>appropriate / relevant / pertinent</u> <u>to cover all areas of / to cover all aspects of</u> the debate in this essay.
- It is <u>beyond the scope of / not within the scope of</u> this report to discuss all aspects of drug abuse. I will focus on …
- I will <u>restrict / confine the discussion to the (narrow) context of</u> law that is made in the courts.
- It is <u>not possible / not feasible</u> here to discuss all the issues surrounding globalisation.
- I will examine here <u>only</u> the two <u>most relevant points / most salient points</u>, namely, pollution and biosphere degradation.
- This report will examine <u>only</u> (the) <u>specific</u> psychological problems attributed to cannabis.

4.2 Information to help you use these words correctly

analyse v **analysis** n	= v – To break something down into its basic elements in order to examine and reveal its important characteristics and/or meaning. (See also section 22, page 145.) ≠ *Analyse, analysis* and *analyses* (US spellings are *analyze, analysis* and *analyses*) *To analyse* is the verb (e.g. I will analyse the data) and analy**sis** is the noun (e.g. We need to do an analy**sis**). *Analy**ses*** is both the third person singular of the verb (e.g. He analyses the results regularly) and the plural noun (e.g. I compared the two analyses). The plural noun is pronounced 'a<u>na</u>lysees'.
argue v **argument** n **arguably** adv **arguable** adj	= v – (1) To use reasoning and evidence to support a statement. This is how *argue* is used in academic study. (2) To disagree with someone or something. n – (1) The process of using evidence and reasoning to support a proposition. This is how *argument* is used in academic study. (2) A quarrel or disagreement. = adv – It can be argued. Similar to *debatably*. (See section 1, page 3.) Use *arguably* to show you are aware that others may disagree or challenge your claim. (See section 27, page 182.) adj – Open to argument or disagreement. Similar to *debatable*.
challenge v / n	= v – In academic study, to disagree with a claim and to try to prove that it is not valid. ⌀ v – To challenge **an assumption // a claim // an idea / a concept // a view**.
concern v / n	= v – To be about or involve. E.g. This essay concerns itself only with therapeutic cloning. n – An issue or problem of interest and importance. ⌀ n – To **cause** concern. **A cause for** concern. **A growing // common** concern. **Widespread** concern. ✳ *To be concerned about* means 'to be worried about' and is too informal to use in academic writing.

contest v / n	= v – To argue against a statement. Similar to *refute*.
	＊ The verb is pronounced cont<u>est</u> and the noun is pronounced <u>cont</u>est.
context n	= The circumstances that form the setting of an event or idea and therefore help us to understand it.
	✐ To **see** / **view** // **place** / **put** the crime **in** its **wider** // **narrower** context. The **social** // **political** // **historical** context **of** a war.
critical adj **criticism** n **criticise** v **critically** adv	= adj – (1) Containing an evaluation of both the positive and negative aspects of something. This is the most common use of *critical* in academic study. E.g. Critical thinking, a critical evaluation. (2) Essential. (3) At an extremely important point and/or a point of crisis.
	＊ *To criticise* usually means to find only fault with something and is therefore not common in academic study. E.g. I will criticise Khan's report … ✘ I will give a critical analysis of Khan's report. ✓
critique v / n	= v – To analyse and evaluate. n – A critical commentary or review, usually in the fields of art or literature.
	≠ *Critique* (n) and *critic* A critique is a written or spoken review of something. The critic is the person who writes the review.
debatably adv	= adv – It can be debated or argued. Similar to *arguably*. (See also section 1, page 3.)
describe v **descriptive** adj	= v – To give an account of something, without analysing, judging or explaining it.

discuss v **discussion** n **discursive** adj	= v – In academic study, to present an argument or issue and then to analyse and evaluate it in a balanced way, revealing the strengths and weaknesses of both sides.
	Gr The noun *discussion* is followed by *about, of, on* or *over*. E.g. There has been much discussion about the crisis. The verb *to discuss* is **not** followed by *about, of, on* or *over*. E.g. I will discuss about censorship. ✗ I will discuss censorship. ✓
	≠ *Discuss* and *debate* *To discuss / A discussion* involves people talking about an issue where the aim is usually to reach agreement rather than to win the argument. *To / A debate* is when people who hold different opinions present their case, usually with the aim of persuading the listeners that the speaker's view is the best or correct one.
elaborate v **elaborate** adj	= v – To give more detailed information or to develop further. adj – Very complicated and/or with many parts. E.g. This is an elaborate design.
enumerate v **enumeration** n	= v – To count out, list, name or give details of.
exploratory adj	= Involving open-minded investigation. In academic writing, an exploratory assignment is one that analyses and discusses information and different viewpoints on the topic or issue.
	≠ *Exploratory, explanatory* and *expository* Explanatory writing explains something else. Examples are explanatory notes or an explanatory paragraph. Expository writing transmits information. Examples of expository writing are directions, instructions and recipes.
feasible adj	= Something that is possible and capable of being done or being dealt with.
	≠ *Feasible* and *likely* *Feasible* is used in the context of plans and projects rather than future predictions. E.g. It is feasible that life on other planets will be discovered. ✗ It is likely / probable that life on other planets will be discovered. ✓

focus v / n	= n – The main object or area of attention. v – To pay particular attention to. *Gr* The plural can be either *focuses* or *foci*. *ℰ* A **broad** // **narrow** // **specific** focus.
pertinent adj	= Relevant or appropriate. *Pertinent* is used when talking about ideas and issues rather than physical objects. *Gr* I will discuss the literature that **is** pertinent **to** clinical application. I will discuss the pertinent literature.
principal adj / n	= adj – The main or most important. ≠ *Principal* and *principle* A princi**ple** is a belief, idea, theory, rule or moral code. E.g. Elections should be based on egalitarian principles.
refute v **refutation** n	= v – To argue against a claim or proposition. Similar to *contest*. n – The act or process of arguing against a proposition.
relevant adj	= Appropriate. Used to refer to subjects, ideas and problems rather than physical objects. Similar to *pertinent*.
salient adj	= The most relevant or important. *ℰ* Salient **points** // **features** // **issues** // **facts** // **properties**.
scope n	= The range of activity, ability, opportunity or possibility. *ℰ* **Within** // **beyond** the scope of this essay. There is **unlimited** // **ample** // **limited** / **restricted** scope. To **broaden** / **widen** / **increase** / **expand** / **extend** // **narrow** / **restrict** the scope.

	speculate v speculation n speculative adj	=	v – (1) In academic work, to introduce an idea or to make a proposition which you then discuss and/or try to prove. (2) To invest in stocks or other financial ventures. n – Discussion and prediction about current and/or future events, often without any evidence.
		Gr	To speculate **that + clause**. E.g. Godolphin speculates that the virus has mutated over the last year. To speculate **on / about + noun**. E.g. Smith speculates on the causes of the disease. To speculate **on / about + what/why/when/whether/how**. E.g. We speculate on how these receptors work.

4.3   Nearly but not quite right

The sentences on the left contain the types of mistakes people make when using words from this section. The correct versions are given on the right.

	Incorrect	Correct
1	It is <u>out of the scope</u> of this essay to analyse all aspects of wealth distribution.	It is <u>beyond the scope</u> of this essay to analyse all aspects of wealth distribution.
2	This study <u>is an analysis about</u> the hyperactive immune system.	This study <u>gives an analysis of</u> the hyperactive immune system.
3	I will <u>discuss about</u> Piaget's theory.	I will <u>discuss</u> Piaget's theory.
4	My essay will <u>consist of</u> the similarities and differences between automatic and conscious ageism.	My essay will <u>examine / discuss</u> the similarities and differences between automatic and conscious ageism.
5	This report <u>focuses around</u> the company BT.	This report <u>focuses on</u> the company BT.
6	Gender is not directly <u>relevant in</u> this issue.	Gender is not directly <u>relevant to</u> this issue.
7	The instruments used were <u>pertinent to</u> the experiment.	The instruments used were <u>appropriate for</u> the experiment.
8	This essay will discuss <u>if</u> there is a connection between wealth and happiness.	This essay will discuss <u>whether</u> there is a connection between wealth and happiness.

	Incorrect	Correct
9	It can be asked how does one measure the quality of life?	The question is how one measures the quality of life.
10	This essay will discuss the topic of whether violent films affect children negatively.	This essay will discuss the issue / question of whether violent films affect children negatively.

5 Talking about proposition, assumption, thesis and theory

This section gives you words and phrases for talking about proposition, assumptions and theory explicitly. Note that talking about propositions and arguments is not the same thing as actually making a proposition or developing an argument yourself. Note also that making an argument cannot be done in a single statement, but requires a process that involves analysing and comparing viewpoints and ideas, evaluating evidence, and drawing conclusions – vocabulary for doing all of this is covered in sections 22 to 28.

5.1 Words in action

Talking about premise and underlying assumption

▸ Creationism is predicated on / is based on the belief that only an intelligent force can explain the complexity of life.
▸ Corporate responsibility presupposes that ethics and the pursuit of profit are compatible.
▸ Democracy is based on the premise / presupposition / assumption that people want choice and freedom.
▸ The (underlying) assumption of // The assumption that underpins biopsychology is that biological, mental and social factors interact.
▸ We can no longer assume that daily newspapers are the most effective print medium for influencing public opinion.

Talking about proposition, thesis, hypothesis and theory (For information on *contend* and *maintain*, see section 24, pages 160–1.)

▸ My assertion // contention // proposition is that law firms must adapt their working practices if they are to meet the challenges of globalisation.
▸ We suggest // propose / posit / postulate a link between low self-esteem and externalising problems.
▸ We assert that / contend that / maintain that there is a link between low self-esteem and externalising problems.
▸ The main thesis of Ritzer's book is that fast-food chains are the most influential example of business rationalisation.
▸ Wood's hypothesis / conjecture is that business and society are interdependent and so jointly responsible for how organisations behave.
▸ Smith is a key figure in biology, known chiefly for his work on the application of game theory to evolutionary biology.

5.2   Information to help you use these words correctly

argue v **argument** n	= v – (1) To use reasoning and evidence to support a statement. This is how *argue* is used in academic study. (2) To disagree with someone or something. n – (1) The process of using evidence and reasoning to support a proposition. This is how *argument* is used in academic study. (2) A quarrel or disagreement.
	≠ *Argument* and *proposition* The word *argument* is sometimes used imprecisely to mean a proposition or contention (see below). Strictly speaking however, an argument is the set and sequence of reasons you use to support a proposition.
	✐ A **convincing / strong // cogent // coherent // plausible / reasonable // reasoned / rational / logical / valid** argument. A **weak // implausible // invalid / flawed / illogical / fallacious** argument.
assertion n **assert** v	= n – A statement of fact or belief. v – To state a fact or belief. (See also section 24, page 158.)
	≠ *Assertion, contention and proposition* These are often used interchangeably but there are some differences in meaning. An *assertion* can include something that is stated but not argued about or tested. A *contention* is something that is argued about, often involving untestable opinion. A *proposition* is something that can be tested or logically proved / disproved. (See below.)

assumption n **assume** v	= n – A fact, idea or belief that is thought to be true but that is not proven. An assumption can be explicitly stated but is usually used to refer to a hidden fact or idea within an argument. An *assumption* is similar to an unstated premise. v – (1) To take for granted. (2) To take on responsibility for, or control of, something.
	≠ *Assumption / assume* and *presumption / presume* Both sets of words mean to take something for granted but they are used in different contexts. *Assumption / assume* are used in the context of academic argument (and also in other contexts, for example, to assume responsibility for something). *Presumption / presume* are not normally used in the context of academic argument. They are used in the context of real life situations involving taking something for granted, acting without authority or acting in an overconfident manner. E.g. People should be presumed innocent. The presumption is that he is dead. They presumed to use my car without asking.
conjecture n	= An opinion or explanation that has not yet been tested, often used in mathematics. Similar to *hypothesis*.
contention n	= A declaration of fact or belief to be argued. Similar to *assertion*. (See above.)
hypothesis n **hypothesise** v **hypothetical** adj	= n – An explanation of how and/or why something happens or will happen, that has yet to be fully tested. A *hypothesis* is a testable, conditional proposition relating to a specific situation (e.g. If X, then Y) even though it may not actually be tested.
	⌀ A **working** hypothesis.
	≠ *Hypothesis, theory* and *thesis* These are sometimes used interchangeably but do have different meanings. See below for *theory* and *thesis*.
posit v	= To put forward a proposition or theory. Similar to *assert, postulate* and *theorise*.
	* *Posit* is less commonly used than *assert, postulate* and *theorise*.

postulate v / n	= v – (1) To put forward a proposition or theory. Similar to *assert, posit* and *theorise*. (2) To assume / To take for granted. n – (1) (In argument) An assumption. (2) A premise / A necessary prerequisite. (3) A self-evident truth. Similar to *axiom*.
predicate v / n	= v – (1) To base on. Used in the context of a proposition and argument. E.g. Our approach is predicated on the evidence of previous studies. (2) To assert something within an argument. This is a much less common use of *to predicate*. ✳ In logic and linguistics, *a predicate / to predicate* have specialised meanings.
premise n	= A proposition used as the basis for an action or argument (the premises are said to 'imply' or 'entail' the conclusion). A form of classical logical argument called a 'syllogism' is where a major and a minor premise form the grounds for the conclusion. E.g. All of her friends are intelligent. Jos is one of her friends, therefore Jos is intelligent.
presuppose v **presupposition** n	= v – To require as a precondition. n – A thing or statement believed, assumed, or needed to exist or be true as a basis for something else. ≠ *Presupposition / presuppose* and *assumption / assume* These can often be interchanged, but there are some differences in meaning. A presupposition is something that must exist or be believed to exist *before* something else can happen. An assumption, however, can be made at any stage of a process or argument. *Presupposition* is therefore a more specific term than *assumption*.

proposition n **propose** v	= n – (1) In an academic context, something declared in a sentence that can be proved or disproved. The proposition is the <u>meaning</u> conveyed in the sentence rather than the form, and therefore different sentences can contain the same proposition. E.g. The world is round. The earth is spherical. The main proposition to be argued is sometimes called an *assertion* or *contention* (see above). The propositions on which the argument is based are the premises. The final proposition in an argument is the conclusion. If the proposition involves a testable explanation of a phenomenon, it is also a hypothesis. (2) In more general contexts, a proposition is an offer or suggestion. v – To suggest / To put forward for consideration a plan or idea. In academic writing *to suggest* is more common than *to propose*. E.g. In this essay I suggest that ethical practice should form a core part of any business. ☍ To propose **a plan // a strategy // a solution // a measure // a policy // reforms // an amendment // legislation.** ≠ *Proposition* and *proposal* These two words have different meanings. A *proposal* is a suggestion or plan (e.g. a proposal for a new transport scheme), not something to be argued.
theory n **theorise** v	= n – A testable (and usually tested) idea or explanation about general principles of the natural world that has been accepted by many experts as the best or one of the best explanations. ≠ *Theory, thesis* and *hypothesis* These three words are sometimes used interchangeably but strictly speaking, they all have distinct meanings. See the entry for *hypothesis* above and for *thesis* below.

thesis n	=	*Thesis* has three related but distinct meanings: (1) A statement of something to be argued or tested, often called a 'thesis statement'. Similar to *proposition*. (2) A hypothesis that is going to be tested or that has already been tested. (3) The written essay, article or book that argues a proposition or tests a hypothesis.
	Gr	The plural of *thesis* is *theses*.
underlying adj underlie n	=	Something hidden and/or existing below the surface. Often used to refer to hidden causes of a surface action, event or belief.
	ℰ	An underlying **assumption** // **belief** // **idea** // **concept** // **principle** // **cause** // **motive** // **reason**.
	≠	*Underlie* and *underpin* These words are not usually interchangeable. Something that *underlies* can be major or minor, positive or negative, valid or invalid. Something that *underpins* is an essential, supporting element. E.g. Government policy is needed to underpin the growth of Irish exports. For *undermine*, see section 12, page 78, and section 16, page 103.

5.3 Nearly but not quite right

The sentences on the left contain the types of mistakes people make when using words from this section. The correct versions are given on the right.

	Incorrect	Correct
1	<u>I want to put forward that</u> major advances in technology require new legislation in order to …	<u>I want to argue / suggest / propose that</u> / <u>My proposition is that</u> major advances in technology require new legislation in order to …
2	I will examine each <u>argument on</u> ID cards in turn.	I will examine each <u>argument for / argument against</u> ID cards in turn.
3	A <u>presumption</u> of the monopolistic competition model is that firms can enter or exit the market freely in response to profit or loss.	An <u>assumption</u> of the monopolistic competition model is that firms can enter or exit the market freely in response to profit or loss.

	Incorrect	Correct
4	My analysis suggests that global central banks will <u>underlie</u> the country's currency in order to avoid financial collapse.	My analysis suggests that global central banks will <u>underpin</u> the country's currency in order to avoid financial collapse.
5	My <u>proposal</u> is that using key performance indicators harms the UK educational system.	My <u>proposition</u> is that key performance indicators harm the UK educational system.
6	Jones and Francis (1996) <u>hypothesis</u> a positive correlation between high self-esteem and a positive attitude to Christianity.	Jones and Francis (1996) <u>hypothesise</u> a positive correlation between high self-esteem and a positive attitude to Christianity.
7	In Great Britain statehood is not <u>predicated with</u> the myth of ethnic homogeneity.	In Great Britain statehood is not <u>predicated on</u> the myth of ethnic homogeneity.
8	From an early stage in his career, Freud <u>speculated on</u> traumatic memories are often repressed.	From an early stage in his career, Freud <u>speculated that</u> traumatic memories are often repressed.
9	Our <u>theory</u> is that the male students will tend to give more positive answers than female students.	Our <u>hypothesis</u> is that the male students will tend to give more positive answers than female students.
10	Without quantum <u>thesis</u> many developments in modern electronics would not have been possible.	Without quantum <u>theory</u> many developments in modern electronics would not have been possible.

Structure, time, sequence and frequency

● ● ● ● ● ●

6 Ordering and structuring your ideas and argument

Presenting and developing your ideas clearly and logically will help to persuade your reader that you know what you are talking about.

Words and phrases sometimes referred to as transition signals or signpost phrases, can help you structure your writing. These include words for adding a similar or contrasting idea (e.g. *similarly, on the other hand* – see section 21), words that show you are making a connection or drawing a conclusion (e.g. *therefore* – see section 26) and words that show you are summarising or restating your argument (e.g. *in conclusion* – see section 28).

Not using signpost phrases or using the wrong ones (for example, using *however* when you mean *in addition*) will confuse your reader and weaken your argument. Remember however, that you should not overuse signpost phrases or try to hide a lack of solid content behind them; good quality research, thinking, ideas and argument are more important than signpost phrases.

Section 6 gives you signpost phrases for explicitly stating the order in which you will present your ideas, for referring to another part of your writing and for moving from one idea to the next. This section also gives you vocabulary that will help you glue together different parts of individual sentences or different parts of your text.

6.1 Words in action

Stating how you intend to order your ideas

▸ This essay will examine three ideas; <u>first, / firstly,</u> ... <u>second, / secondly,</u> ... <u>finally,</u> ...

▸ We report on neuropeptide Y and peptide YY as possible markers for depression and schizophrenia <u>respectively</u>.

▸ An overview of the legislation is <u>followed by</u> a critical evaluation of the proposed amendments.

▸ <u>Following</u> an overview of the legislation, I will critically evaluate the proposed amendments.

▸ I will examine the impact of the Employment Act 2008, and <u>in addition</u> will discuss possible future amendments.

- I will <u>also / additionally</u> give examples of how a translator can work with an author to enhance a text.
- I will discuss this issue <u>further</u> when I look at multinational corporations.
- <u>Further / Additional</u> analysis will be given in section two.

Moving from one idea to the next

Ideas that support each other

- The translator may not understand the author's main intention. <u>In addition to this, / Additionally, / Furthermore, / Moreover,</u> they may not have sufficient grasp of the original language to convey small differences in meaning.
- The previous paragraph outlined the main sources of automatic ageism. There are <u>also</u> several other more minor sources.

Ideas that contrast with each other

- Relief theory states that humour has developed to reduce tension. Superiority theory <u>however, / on the other hand,</u> suggests that humour is used chiefly to assert superiority. The latter concept …
- Criminal law aims to uphold national standards of behaviour. <u>In contrast to this, / By contrast,</u> civil law exists to protect individuals against each other. Civil law …

Moving on to a different idea

- There is little evidence that actual poverty in the UK is increasing. <u>With regard to / Regarding / As regards / In respect of / With respect to / Concerning / As for / Moving on to</u> relative poverty, …
- <u>Turning now to / If we turn now to / If we look now at</u> reproductive cloning rather than therapeutic, evidence suggests that …
- <u>Leaving aside</u> the issue of structured training, normal daily physical activity is a neglected area. Daily exercise can …

Referring to other parts of your writing

- The theory of special relativity outlined <u>above</u> was superseded by that of general relativity.
- The diagram <u>below</u> shows the decrease in infection from aerobic and anaerobic bacteria.
- The <u>previous / preceding</u> paragraph outlined the main sources of ageism. There are also, however, other …
- Chapter one deals with small businesses. <u>Subsequent</u> chapters look at large businesses and …
- In the <u>following</u> section I analyse the data collected and discuss some possible implications.

Referring to ideas in a previous sentence or within a sentence (See also appendix, pages 203–4 on using *this* and *these*.)

▸ Much of Freud's collection was uncontroversial, but he also had 'shameful' pieces. <u>The former</u> were publicly displayed while <u>the latter</u> were not.

▸ It is important to distinguish between actual and relative poverty, and I will argue that the <u>former</u> concept is less relevant.

▸ People experience happiness more often than unpleasant emotions but <u>the latter</u> have a greater impact on …

▸ The Fisher-Race and the Wiener systems are referred to here as CDE and Rh-Hr <u>respectively</u>.

▸ <u>The following</u> countries joined the European Union in 2004: the Czech Republic, Cyprus, …

6.2 Information to help you use these words correctly

following adj / prep / n	=	adj – Coming next in time or order. E.g. In the following section I analyse … prep – After that / subsequently. E.g. Following the Potsdam Agreement, Germans were expelled from Poland.
	≠	*Following* (adj) and *forthcoming* *Forthcoming* means going to happen or come soon, rather than next. E.g. The forthcoming elections in May will be important.
former adj	=	(1) The first item mentioned in a list (usually of only two items). E.g. From a choice of **happiness** or health, 86% of participants chose the **former**. (2) Having existed in the past.
further adj / adv	=	adv – Additional / more. E.g. Further details will be given next week.
	≠	*Further* and *farther* *Further* is used as an adjective and adverb to mean 'more / additionally' for both physical distance and capacity. E.g. adj – Jupiter is further from the Sun than Venus. adv – I can't walk any further. adv – I discuss this further in the next section. adv – The business can't develop further. *Farther* is much less common and is only used to refer to physical distance. E.g. Jupiter is farther from the Sun than Venus. ✓ I can't walk any farther. ✓ I discuss this farther in the next section. ✗ The business can't develop farther. ✗

furthermore adv	=	*Furthermore* means 'also' and is used to give an additional point in a discussion or argument.
latter adj	=	(1) The second of two things mentioned. E.g. They looked at peptides Y and **YY** and found that **the latter** is a marker for schizophrenia. (2) The last stages of a process or time period. Similar to one meaning of *later*. E.g. In the latter / later stages of growth the term 'foetus' is used rather than 'embryo'.
moving on to	*Gr*	In formal writing *moving on* must be followed by **to**.
precede v **preceding** adj	=	v – To happen or go immediately before. (See also section 7, page 46 for *precede, predate* and *proceed*.)
regard n / v	=	v – To consider or think of something or someone in a particular way. See also section 19, page 116. n – (1) Care or attention given to something or someone. (2) With reference or connection to something or someone. E.g. In regard to ethics, I will show that …
	Gr	n – **As** regards ethics, … ✓ **In** regard **to** ethics, … ✓ **In** regard**s** **to** ethics, … ✗
respectively adv **respective** adj	=	adv – Separately and in the same order as the items just mentioned. E.g. The <u>Fisher-Race</u> and the **Wiener** systems are referred to as <u>CDE</u> and **Rh-Hr** respectively. (See also section 3, page 17.)
	≠	*Respectively* and *respective* *Respectively* is used to emphasise the order and relation of different items in a sentence. *Respective* emphasises the difference and separateness of the things mentioned. E.g. Each candidate had their respective merits and so it was difficult to decide who should get the job.
subsequent adj **subsequently** adv	=	adj – Existing or happening afterwards.
	≠	*Subsequent* and *consequent* *Consequent* means happening afterwards <u>as a result of</u> the previous event.

6.3 Nearly but not quite right

The sentences on the left contain the types of mistakes people make when using words from this section. The correct versions are given on the right.

	Incorrect	Correct
1	The media and the public are both factors. The <u>later one</u> however, is the most influential.	The media and the public are both factors. The <u>latter</u> however, is the most influential.
2	Sroufe (1979) looked at how level of care in early childhood affects <u>following</u> development in adolescence.	Sroufe (1979) looked at how level of care in early childhood affects <u>subsequent</u> development in adolescence.
3	The <u>forthcoming</u> quotation illustrates the view that academic language has important similarities to a foreign language: "…	The <u>following</u> quotation illustrates the view that academic language has important similarities to a foreign language: "…
4	<u>In the first place</u> I will summarise current research in this area and then …	<u>First / Firstly</u>, I will summarise current research in this area and then …
5	In her discussion summarised <u>earlier on</u>, Smith fails to consider all possible circumstances.	In her discussion summarised <u>above</u>, Smith fails to consider all possible circumstances.
6	<u>Staying on the point of</u> logins, passwords can be reset every 72 days.	<u>Continuing with / Staying on the subject of</u> logins, passwords can be reset every 72 days.
7	<u>Further will be considered</u> alternative methods of making mobile technology more secure.	Alternative methods of making mobile technology more secure will <u>also</u> be considered. (Meaning 'in addition'.) Alternative methods of making mobile technology more secure <u>will be considered further</u> in the next section. (Meaning 'in more detail'.)
8	<u>Moving on,</u> job satisfaction Cote and Morgan state that this is influenced by the presence of pleasant emotions at work.	<u>Moving on to</u> job satisfaction, Cote and Morgan state that this is influenced by the presence of pleasant emotions at work.
9	<u>To refer to</u> the *New Scientist*, this journal successfully simplifies complex concepts.	<u>With regard to / As regards / Regarding / In respect of / Concerning</u> the *New Scientist*, it successfully simplifies complex concepts.

	Incorrect	Correct
10	<u>In the aspect of</u> violent computer games, several recent studies have been conducted.	<u>With regard to / As regards / Regarding / In respect of / Concerning</u> violent computer games, several recent studies have been conducted.

7   Time, sequence, duration and frequency

7.1   Words in action

Time: past, present and looking back

‣ I will give an overview of <u>past / previous</u> studies.
‣ Mumbai was <u>formerly / previously</u> known as Bombay.
‣ Sadat is a <u>former</u> president of Egypt.
‣ <u>As yet / So far / Up to now</u> there has been no narrowing of the pay gap.
‣ There has been no narrowing of the pay gap <u>as yet / so far / up to now</u>.
‣ The <u>current</u> situation is not sustainable.
‣ I will contrast attitudes to crime in <u>contemporary</u> and in late Victorian society.
‣ The discussion over the safety of the mumps vaccine is <u>ongoing</u>.
‣ Significant changes in the way food is delivered and sold <u>are underway</u> in Asia.
‣ <u>With hindsight / In retrospect</u> it would have been better to use a much larger sample.

Time: future and first occurrence

‣ Two species of cetacean are in danger of <u>imminent</u> extinction.
‣ It is worth asking whether <u>future</u> studies should follow the same procedure.
‣ <u>The advent of / The arrival of</u> cellular technology enabled widespread use of mobile phones.
‣ The ZUP party's election is being hailed in the media as an <u>unprecedented</u> success.

Sequence of events

‣ The <u>chronology of</u> the Chinese dynasties is well-documented.
‣ Evidence indicates that the Chicxulub crater <u>antedates / predates</u> the KT mass extinction.
‣ Everett <u>preceded</u> Lincoln at the 1863 dedication ceremony of the <u>National Cemetery.</u>
‣ The current regime has so far proved to be less radical than the <u>previous</u> one.
‣ A white paper usually states policy intention <u>prior to</u> a new piece of legislation.
‣ Turing's machine was a <u>forerunner of / precursor to</u> the modern personal computer.
‣ Brown (1991) points out that <u>successive</u> governments have tried to modify pay settlements.
‣ This report gives an <u>interim</u> analysis until the final report is published next year.
‣ Heat transfer between the fluid and cylinder head is <u>instantaneous</u>.
‣ The two earthquakes were <u>simultaneous</u> even though 500 miles apart.

- It is useful to run two browsers <u>concurrently / simultaneously</u> in order to access all websites.
- A fall in price is often <u>accompanied by</u> an increase in demand.
- During the interview we <u>alternated</u> between direct and indirect questions.
- The study found that a decrease in HRT <u>coincided with</u> a decrease in breast tumours.
- Hangen et al. (2012) look at the effect of stock price volatility on <u>subsequent</u> return expectations.
- The theory of special relativity was <u>superseded</u> by that of general relativity.

Duration

- There is a lack of research on <u>the duration of</u> depressive episodes in teenagers.
- We will examine the <u>short-</u>, <u>medium-</u> and <u>long-term</u> effects of post-traumatic stress.
- We decided to <u>extend / prolong</u> the interviews with the younger participants.
- According to the survey, high-end hotels have a relatively large number of <u>transient / temporary</u> employees.
- From April 2007, applicants for <u>permanent</u> residence in the UK have had to take a <u>'Life in the UK' test</u>.
- They have agreed to keep their currency fixed <u>for an indefinite period / indefinitely</u>.
- The debate over the status of social work has been running <u>throughout</u> this century.
- Negotiations were <u>suspended</u> during the local elections.
- There was a <u>hiatus</u> in the negotiations during the local elections.

Frequency

- There were <u>frequent // regular // infrequent / occasional</u> tremors.
- There were <u>recurrent</u> outbreaks of plague in Europe in the thirteenth century.
- The government made <u>repeated</u> efforts to resolve the Bougainville conflict.
- The study found that cancer <u>recurred</u> in 23% of patients.
- Producing <u>periodic</u> progress reports is good business practice.
- Our data confirm(s) the <u>continuous</u> growth in the sector up to October 2012.
- Negotiations on carbon emissions will <u>continue</u> at the summit next year.
- The problem of <u>intermittent</u> internet connection is often related to broadband capacity.
- The virus outbreak seems to have been an <u>isolated</u> incident.
- True genius is <u>a rarity / rare</u>.

7.2 Information to help you use these words correctly

alternate v / n **alternate** adj	= v – To move back and forth between two things or conditions. = adj – Every other (of two things). E.g. He worked alternate weeks. ≠ *Alternate* and *alternative* *An alternative* is a noun meaning another option or possibility. E.g. If this strategy fails to work there are alternative approaches we can take. ∗ The verb is pronounced <u>a</u>lternate and the adjective is pronounced al<u>ter</u>nate.
chronology n **chronological** adj	= n – The order in which past or present events happen.
concurrent adj **concurrently** adv	= adj – Occurring or existing at the same time. Similar to *simultaneously*. Often used in mechanical, scientific and operational contexts. E.g. We ran the two programs concurrently.
contemporary adj / n **contemporaneous** adj	= adj – (1) Modern or current. E.g. Many contemporary artists use mixed media. (2) Done or existing together in the same time period (months / years). Similar to *contemporaneous*. E.g. The diary is a contemporary / contemporaneous account of the 1912 riots. A fall in price is often contemporaneous with / accompanied by an increase in demand. n – A person living at the same time mentioned. E.g. Shelley and Byron were contemporaries. ∗ The fact that the adjective *contemporary* has the two different meanings above can cause ambiguity. *Contemporary* is usually used to mean 'modern' and *contemporaneous* to mean 'of the same time period'.

continual adj **continually** adv	= adj – Happening frequently but with interruptions. Similar to *constant*. * Often used for negative things. E.g. The country suffered continual wars. We had continual problems. ≠ *Continual* and *continuous* These words can be interchangeable but *continual* is used to emphasise stopping and starting, while *continuous* emphasises continuity and is often used for positive things. (See below.)
continue v **continued** adj	= v – To keep doing, to resume or to carry something forward. E.g. We continue to learn throughout our lives. This is to be continued tomorrow. The continued existence of our planet is essential.
continuous adj	= Happening or existing over time, often (but not always) without interruption. * Often used for positive things. E.g. Continuous assessment. Continuous growth. ≠ *Continuous* and *continual* – see above.
current adj **currently** adv	= (1) Existing or happening now or during the time period being discussed. (2) A movement or force, e.g. an electrical current or charge. ≠ *Current* and *currant* A currant is a dried grape.

former adj **formerly** adv	= adj – Of or happening in the past.
	≠ *Formerly* and *Formally* *Formally* means done in a traditional and/or official manner. E.g. We haven't been formally introduced.
	≠ *Former/ly* and *previous/ly* There is some overlap between the two words but there are also some important differences in usage. *Former/ly* is usually used to talk about names, titles and positions whereas *previous* is a more everyday word used to describe the sequence of events in time. E.g. The book's title is 'The Country Formerly Known as Great Britain'. This report is similar to one I've read previously.
	* With both *former/ly* and *previous/ly*, using *the* with the key noun gives the meaning of 'the one immediately before now' and using *a* gives the less specific meaning of 'one of the former / previous'. E.g. Lockhart is <u>the</u> former director of the college = the director that preceded the current one. Birch is <u>a</u> former director of the college = one of the former directors.
hindsight n	= An understanding or realisation of something only after it has happened.
	Gr **With** hindsight.
imminent adj	= About to happen or likely to happen very soon.
	≠ *Imminent* and *eminent* *Eminent* means notable, admired and respected. Often used to describe someone who is an expert in their field. (See section 16, page 99.)
	≠ *Imminent*, *immanent* and *immanant* *Imminent* means about to happen or likely to happen very soon (as stated above). *Immanent* means 'naturally part of something' or 'existing within', usually used in philosophy and religion. *Immanant* is a mathematical term relating to the properties of a matrix.

instantaneous adj	=	Happening or done with almost no time delay.
	*	*Instantaneous* and the adjective *instant* (*instant* can also be a noun as in the phrase 'in an instant') have similar meanings but *instantaneous* is the more formal word often used in academic contexts.
intermittent adj	=	Happening irregularly, with frequent stopping and starting.
isolated adj	=	(1) Happening only once. (2) Geographically distant from areas of habitation. (3) Lonely.
	⌀	(1) An isolated **case / incidence of / incident / occurrence / outbreak / phenomenon**.
past n / adj	≠	*Past* and *passed* *Past* means 'before now'. E.g. Past studies indicate that … *Passed* is the past form of the verb *to pass*. E.g. Oral traditions are passed down from generation to generation.
periodic adj	=	Regular but not frequent.
precede v	=	To happen or go before in time, order or position.
	≠	*Proceed* and *precede* To *proceed* is to go forward or to keep doing something, often towards a particular goal.
precursor n	=	Something that comes before something else of a similar type and influences it in an important way.
predate v	=	(1) To happen or exist before something else, often with the meaning of 'to be older than'. (2) To mark with a date earlier than the actual one. E.g. To predate a cheque.
	*	Strictly speaking, the correct word for meaning (1) is *antedate*.
prior adj / prep	=	Existing or coming before in time, order, or importance. Similar to *previous* but more formal, and only *prior* is used as a preposition. E.g. I had a prior / previous arrangement. I added the liquid prior to / before heating. ✓ I added the liquid previous to heating. ✗

prolong v	$=$ To extend the amount of time.
	e To prolong **life** // **life expectancy** // **survival** // **suffering** // **conflict** // **a visit** // **an exam** // **an interview** // **a meeting**.
recur v	$=$ v – To happen again.
recurrent adj	
retrospect n	$=$ A review of something after it has happened. Similar to *hindsight*.
	Gr **in** retrospect
subsequent adj	$=$ Coming after, following.
successive adj	$=$ Existing or happening one after another (in a series).
supersede v	$=$ To take the place of.
	✳ The spelling is supersede not supercede.
underway adj	$=$ Recently started.
unprecedented adj	$=$ Never happened before, or the greatest yet in size, degree or importance.
	✳ The word *precedented* is rarely used. The opposite of *unprecedented* would be a word such as *unimportant*, *ordinary* or *unremarkable*.

7.3 Nearly but not quite right

The sentences on the left contain the types of mistakes people make when using words from this section. The correct versions are given on the right.

	Incorrect	Correct
1	They are planning to cut costs <u>in</u> the wrong time.	They are planning to cut costs <u>at</u> the wrong time.
2	The experiments have been <u>undergoing</u> for five years.	The experiments have been <u>ongoing</u> for five years.
3	Animal testing <u>has been proceeding</u> for a long time.	Animal testing <u>has existed / has been happening</u> for a long time.

	Incorrect	Correct
4	<u>As of today,</u> the UK government <u>is currently</u> tackling gun crime.	The UK government <u>is currently</u> tackling gun crime.
5	We conducted the experiments on <u>alternative</u> days so that we could analyse the data each time.	We conducted the experiments on <u>alternate</u> days so that we could analyse the data each time.
6	<u>Within</u> two years the figures <u>have continued</u> to rise.	<u>Over the last / Over the past</u> two years the figures <u>have continued</u> to rise. or The figures <u>have been</u> rising <u>for</u> two years.
7	As the years have <u>developed</u> we have seen an increase in relative poverty.	As the years have <u>passed</u> we have seen an increase in relative poverty.
8	The interviews were conducted <u>previous to</u> giving out the questionnaire.	The interviews were conducted <u>before / prior to</u> giving out the questionnaire.
9	Animal cloning has been an area of research <u>for modern</u> years.	Animal cloning <u>has been</u> // <u>has become</u> an area of research <u>in recent</u> years.
10	Recreational drugs <u>use to</u> be almost encouraged in certain professions.	Recreational drugs <u>used to</u> be almost encouraged in certain professions.

Methodology and method, findings, size, amount, level and proportion

● ● ● ● ● ●

8 Describing your methodology and method

When describing method and process it is common to use the passive form (e.g. The data was (were) collected …). If you have performed the action on your own, use the active form (e.g. I collected the data …), and save *we* for when you are referring to teamwork.

8.1 Words in action

Methodology

▸ As I was investigating my own teaching, my <u>methodology</u> was based on practice-based research.
▸ <u>We chose to use</u> case studies <u>to address our research question</u> in order to …
▸ <u>I decided that an</u> exploratory approach would be <u>an effective way of</u> assessing the scope of research needed.
▸ <u>A</u> comparative expression <u>analysis</u> <u>enabled us to</u> identify the relevant gene regions.
▸ <u>Working with</u> data over a wide area <u>allowed us to</u> use a <u>statistical analysis</u>.
▸ <u>We used</u> anonymous questionnaires <u>so as not to</u> cause offence if the feedback was negative.
▸ I first analysed the <u>empirical data</u>, and then used <u>qualitative methods</u> to gain additional information on individuals.
▸ We used both <u>quantitative and qualitative</u> <u>measures</u> to determine the effects of the programme.

Method

▸ The intervention <u>took the form of</u> two half-day visits each term.
▸ We agreed the <u>format</u> of the experiment beforehand.
▸ We used <u>systematic</u> sampling to select participants.
▸ The participants were <u>allocated / assigned</u> randomly to one of five groups.
▸ Each participant <u>was subjected to / underwent</u> a series of four tests.

- The experiment was <u>repeated</u> by other teams to see whether our results could be <u>replicated / reproduced</u>.
- We <u>collated</u> the sets of figures at the end of each week.
- We then <u>compiled</u> a database and used it to look for significant correlations.
- We <u>collaborated</u> with a team of researchers from Glasgow.
- The study <u>involved</u> interviewing participants after each intervention.

Stages or process

- <u>Prior to / Before</u> measuring the solution we <u>extracted</u> the blood cells.
- <u>Once</u> a patch of pink begins to appear in the solution, the tap will be stopped.
- The <u>first // next // penultimate // final step</u> in the process was to …
- <u>At // During</u> the <u>initial // intermediate // final stage / phase</u> we …
- <u>At each stage we</u> <u>monitored // observed</u> the behaviour of the animals.
- This <u>complex sequence of</u> experiments was completed in 28 hours.

Requirements, parameters, limits and limitations

- We followed closely the instructions <u>stipulated / specified</u> in the written protocol.
- Owing to time <u>constraints</u> we were only able to repeat the test once.
- My aim was to find the lower <u>limit</u> detection value for the drug.
- Both sexes showed a lower pain <u>threshold</u> in the third session.
- We were <u>limited as to</u> how much we could achieve in the time given.
- The employer put <u>limitations</u> on where we could conduct the interviews.
- We ensured that all values were <u>within the specific / the specified parameters</u>

8.2 Information to help you use these words correctly

allocate v	= v – To give or assign to a specific group or for a specific purpose.
allocated adj	✐ v – To allocate **funds / funding // money // resources**.
collate v	= To collect and put together in order to analyse.

compile v	= To create something by bringing information together.
	≠ *Compile* and *collate* *To compile* means to create something you didn't have before. E.g. From the data we collated, I compiled <u>a list of</u> all students who had attended the meeting.
constraint n	= Something that puts limits on something else. Similar to *limitations*.
	Gr To **work within** constraints.
	⊘ To work within **financial // economic // legal // time // budgetary** constraints.
effective adj	= Having the desired outcome / effect.
	≠ *Effective* and *efficient* *Efficient* means making the best possible use of time, effort, energy, money etc. Something can therefore be effective (successful) but not use resources well and so be inefficient. Equally, something might use resources well (be efficient) but ultimately fail to have the desired result and so be ineffective.
extract v / n	= v – To take or remove something out of something else, often using force. E.g. The proteins were extracted from the liquid. n – A section of a book, film, piece of music etc. E.g. He read an extract from the novel.
	* The verb is pronounced extr<u>a</u>ct and the noun is pronounced <u>e</u>xtract.
limit n / v	= n – The furthest extent or boundary that is allowed or is possible. v – To restrict.
limitation n	= (1) A rule, restriction or situation that restricts something. (2) A failing or deficiency. E.g. The novels are important but they have limitations.
limited adj	= (1) Restricted in some way. (2) Of people, narrow minded or lacking in ability.

methodology n **methodological** adj	= n – The principles and general approach or system used in an area of research.
	≠ *Methodology* and *method* A *methodology* is the explanation, evaluation and discussion of the method, or collection of methods, chosen to form a framework that addresses the research question. A *method* is a particular procedure within the overall research framework. *Methodological* and *methodical* *Methodological* relates to a methodology. E.g. This essay will examine the methodological foundations of market research. *Methodical* means organised and thorough and/or done following an established procedure. E.g. The job requires someone who can work in a methodical manner.
parameter n	= (1) The boundaries or specifications that limit and shape what can be done. (2) A measurable quality or value.
	Gr Often used in the plural and often with *the*.
	⌀ To **set** // **define** // **establish** // **determine** the parameters. To **change** / **adjust** / **modify** // **vary** the parameters. To **fall** // **operate** / **work within** the (specified) parameters. **Certain** / **specific** // **specified** // **broad** // **strict** parameters.
	≠ *Parameter* and *perimeter* A *perimeter* is the outer edge of a prison, field, football pitch or other delineated area.
penultimate adj	= The one before last in a series.
qualitative adj	= Any research method that gathers information (e.g. attitudes, feelings or beliefs) that cannot be expressed in, or reduced to, numerical values. Examples of qualitative methods are participant observation and interviews.
quantitative adj	= Any research method that collects empirical (observable), numerical or statistical data. A quantitative approach is part of what is referred to as the scientific method.

sequence n / v	= n – The order in which a (planned or unplanned) set of events happen or set of items occur.
stage n / v	= n – A particular point within a process.
step n / v	= n – A specific action within a process.
stipulate v **stipulation** n	= v – To specify, require, demand or necessitate. See also section 20, page 131. 🖉 The **model** // **regulations** // **rules** // **law** // **contract** // **instructions** // **standards** // **doctrine** // **policy** stipulate(s) that ...
systematic adj	= According to a particular system, method or plan. 🖉 A systematic **approach** // **classification** // **course**. ≠ *Systematic* and *systemic* *Systemic* means relating to, or spread throughout, a whole system or organism. E.g. A systemic disease, effect, risk, problem or failure. (See also section 14, page 88.)
undergo v	= To experience something (often bad or unpleasant) or to go through a process of change. 🖉 To undergo **surgery** // **treatment** // **testing** // **pain** // **hardship** // **suffering**. To undergo **transformation** // **revision** / **modification** // **repair** // **restructuring**.

8.3 Nearly but not quite right

The sentences on the left contain the types of mistakes people make when using words from this section. The correct versions are given on the right.

	Incorrect	Correct
1	The process <u>to produce</u> the waste is complicated.	The process <u>of producing</u> the waste is complicated.
2	This is an ineffective method <u>to determine the cause</u>.	This is an ineffective method <u>of determining</u> the cause.
3	Researchers <u>are undergoing studies about</u> the possible effects of the drug.	Researchers are <u>conducting studies on</u> the possible effects of the drug.

	Incorrect	Correct
4	The survey was <u>done</u> in six cities.	The survey was <u>conducted</u> in six cities.
5	The process <u>continuous</u> until the urine reaches the second tubule.	The process <u>continues</u> until the urine reaches the second tubule.
6	This one-stage process <u>includes</u> removing a small disc of material.	This one-stage process <u>involves</u> removing a small disc of material.
7	The removal of waste products from the blood is a vital <u>sequence</u>.	The removal of waste products from the blood is a vital <u>process.</u>
8	Klun argues that animals should not <u>take part in</u> such experiments.	Klun argues that animals should not <u>be subjected to / undergo</u> such experiments.
9	We then <u>compiled</u> the answers from the questionnaires.	We then <u>collated</u> the answers from the questionnaires.
10	We were careful not to exceed the agreed time <u>limitation</u>.	We were careful not to exceed the agreed time <u>limit</u>.

9 Presenting initial data and findings, and stating problems and anomalies

See also sections 11 and 12 for movement and change, section 20 for cause and effect, and section 26 for drawing conclusions.

9.1 Words in action

Initial data and findings

- This report presents our initial // provisional findings.
- The table // chart shows the data obtained.
- No (significant) change // rise // fall was detected // was observed.
- We discerned differences in patterns of behaviour between the two groups.
- The data show(s) a statistically significant cluster of birth defects in the region.
- The participants exhibited signs of nervousness such as coughing.
- We found that male–female wage disparity varies with age.
- Our excavation has yielded important new evidence of habitation.
- The data accord(s) / agree(s) / is (are) consistent with our earlier observations.
- The distribution pattern of the virus conforms to that expected for this type of disease.
- At this preliminary stage of analysis the findings are inconclusive / not conclusive.

Problems

- We encountered a problem with the software and so had to do the calculations manually.
- We were unable to replicate our results, even though / despite the fact that / in spite of the fact that we repeated the experiment six times.
- We found that the sample was too small to produce a measurable outcome.
- I found that I had overestimated // underestimated the effect unemployment has on happiness.
- Our procedure was more fallible than we thought and we had to abandon the experiment.

Anomalies and surprises

- There were several anomalies in the data, which means that we need to repeat the experiment.
- There was an unexplained discrepancy between the expected and actual totals.
- The discrepancy exceeded an acceptable margin of error.
- Our results were not consistent with / inconsistent with the predicted outcomes.

- A <u>notable</u> <u>exception to</u> rising export prices was Mexico.
- The standard of answers was higher // lower <u>than</u> we had <u>anticipated / expected // predicted</u>.
- The data do (does) <u>not accord with / not agree with</u> our <u>earlier observations</u>.
- <u>Contrary to (our / my) expectations</u>, the most effective type of bulb was also the cheapest.

9.2   Information to help you use these words correctly

accord v / n **accordance** n	=	v – (1) To be consistent with or the same as. (2) To give or grant (status or respect) to someone.
	Gr	v – (1) X accords **with** Y. n – X **is in** accordance **with** Y. For *according to*, see section 23, page 152.
anomaly n **anomalous** adj	=	n – Something that is different from what is usual, expected or normal.
conform v **conformity** n	=	v – (1) To behave according to generally accepted social patterns or standards. (See section 14, page 86.) (2) To be similar to an already established type, form or idea. E.g. The restaurant conforms to people's idea of a family business.
	Gr	To **conform to** X.
	≠	*Conform* and *consistent* These words do have some overlap. However, *conform* means more than *consistent* (is similar to) because *conform* means that something is consistent with an already established phenomenon or idea.
consistent adj	=	(1) Does not contradict. (2) Unchanging over time.
	Gr	X is consistent **with** Y.
	⌀	A consistent **approach** // **standard** // **level**. X is consistent with the **aim** // **data** // **evidence** // **findings** // **objective** // **principle** // **view** of Y. X is **broadly** // **wholly** consistent with Y.

datum / data n	=	Statistics, facts or other information to be analysed.
	Gr	In formal scientific writing, *datum* is the singular noun and *data* is the plural noun. E.g. The input **datum is** incomplete. The **data are** from three different sources. However, using *data* as a singular uncountable noun is now common. E.g. The **data is** shown in Figure 1.
detect v **detection** n	=	v – To discover the presence of something.
	≠	*Detect* and *discern* These words can sometimes be interchanged, but *discern* tends to be used when the presence is small, subtle and therefore difficult to see or recognise. *Discern* is also used in a narrower range of contexts than *detect* – see below.
discern v **discernible** adj	=	v – To recognise, find or understand something, often when the thing discerned is not immediately obvious. Usually used in the context of something visual or intellectual.
	🖉	To discern a (an) / A discernible **difference** // **change** // **shift** // **link** // **trend** // **relationship** // **pattern** // **theme** // **impact** // **effect** // **influence** // **benefit**.
discrepancy n	=	A difference between two or more things that are expected to be the same.
disparity n	=	A significant and/or large difference between two or more things.
distribution n	=	(1) The way something is spread, shared out or present over a given area. (2) The process of transporting and delivering goods to buyers or customers.
	✳	In mathematics, *distribution* has a more specialised meaning.
	🖉	**Equal** // **even** // **uneven** // **narrow** // **wide** distribution.

exception n **except** conj / prep	= n – Different in some way from the other things mentioned. ⊘ n – A **notable** // **rare** // **odd** // **obvious** exception. The **only** / **sole** exception. ≠ *Exception* and *exemption* An *exemption* is permission to ignore a rule. ✳ The adjective and adverb *exceptional* and *exceptionally* have a different meaning, that of being unique and/or outstanding. E.g. This is an exceptionally good piece of work.
fallible adj **fallibility** n	= adj – Vulnerable to being wrong or to making errors.
findings n	= Facts, statistics or other types of information. ≠ *Findings, data* and *results* *Findings* is the most general word of the three and is used to refer to both data and results. *Data* is a more specific term than *findings*. *Data* is information (particularly numerical) collected for calculation, analysis and decision-making. *Results* is sometimes used to refer to data but *results* should really be used to refer to the observations, inferences and conclusions drawn <u>from</u> the data.
initial adj	= First, at the beginning. In the context of findings and results, *initial* can also have the meaning of incomplete.
notable n	= Interesting and important. ⊘ A notable **exception** // **absence** // **difference** // **omission**. A notable **achievement** // **accomplishment** // **success** // **contribution** // **example** // **feature**. ≠ *Notable* and *noticeable* *Noticeable* means 'easily seen'. Something that is noticeable might not be interesting or important (notable) and something that is notable might not be easily seen.
provisional adj	= Not final, and liable to be changed, or incomplete.

| | yield v / n | = | v – (1) To produce or generate. (2) To give way to something or someone. |
| | | | n – The amount produced or generated. |

9.3 Nearly but not quite right

The sentences on the left contain the types of mistakes people make when using words from this section. The correct versions are given on the right.

	Incorrect	Correct
1	We have to <u>analysis</u> the results.	We have to <u>analyse</u> the results.
2	These statistics were <u>carried out</u> for two specific purposes.	These statistics were <u>produced / gathered</u> for two specific purposes.
3	The participants' scores were <u>of higher expectations</u>.	The participants' scores were <u>higher than expected.</u>
4	A larger sample will result in a lower margin <u>for</u> error.	A larger sample will result in a lower margin <u>of</u> error.
5	Our results <u>accorded to</u> those of the other research teams.	Our results <u>accorded with</u> those of the other research teams.
6	The table <u>contains various statistical facts</u> from our initial analysis.	The table contains <u>statistics</u> from our initial analysis.
7	The database <u>complied</u> from the statistics is shown in Table 2.	The database <u>compiled</u> from the statistics is shown in Table 2.
8	There are several <u>disparities</u> between the original report and the summary given in the journal.	There are several <u>discrepancies</u> between the original report and the summary given in the journal.
9	<u>Minority groups have been overestimated when concerning gun crime.</u>	<u>The proportion / number / percentage of people from minority groups involved in gun crime has been overestimated.</u>
10	With one <u>exemption</u>, the participants chose the most expensive item.	With one <u>exception</u>, the participants chose the most expensive item.

10 Size, amount, level, capacity, proportion and ratio

This section gives words and phrases for discussing number and data in non-specialised academic contexts. It contains words and phrases for approximate amounts (e.g. *a large number of*) but you will also probably need to use precise numerical values when discussing data in your own writing.

See also section 15 for words related to 'not enough' and 'too much'.

10.1 Words in action

Size and amount

▶ The pay increase had a <u>minimal / negligible</u>
<u>small</u>
<u>noticeable / appreciable</u>
<u>considerable / marked / major / significant / substantial / pronounced</u>
effect on output.

▶ Over the last decade there has been a <u>profound</u> change in the way charities advertise their work.
▶ There are <u>numerous</u> planets as yet undetected in the galaxy.
▶ There are <u>few</u> studies on the impact of age and gender on peptide levels.
▶ There were <u>a number of / several</u> options the government could have taken.
▶ <u>A large numer of // A small number of</u> students returned the questionnaire.
▶ There was <u>a large amount of // a small amount of</u> CO_2 in the chamber.
▶ <u>A total of</u> 305 questionnaires were completed.

Measurement

▶ The experiment was designed to <u>quantify / measure</u> the relative levels of male and female participation.

Level, capacity and dimension

▶ Supernovas of type la are considered to have <u>maximum</u> brightness.
▶ Harmonised <u>minimum safety levels / minimum levels of safety</u> are essential for European transport networks.
▶ We used electronic scales to ensure a high <u>level of / degree of</u> accuracy.
▶ This type of cartridge <u>has a maximum</u> <u>capacity of</u> 800 GB. / The <u>maximum</u> <u>capacity of</u> this type of cartridge <u>is</u> 800 GB.
▶ Scores above 110 indicate <u>a higher than average / an above-average</u> IQ, and scores under 90 indicate <u>a lower than average / a below-average</u> <u>level</u> of intelligence.

- ‣ Wallace and Wallace (1998) argue that the costs of student evaluations <u>exceed</u> their value.
- ‣ The diagram gives the <u>approximate</u> dimensions of the fan (i.e. to the nearest centimetre).

Proportion, fraction and ratio

- ‣ Average propensity to save (APS) is the <u>proportion of</u> income saved rather than spent.
- ‣ The UK Sentencing Council states that a sentence should be <u>in proportion to / proportionate to</u> the crime.
- ‣ <u>Proportional</u> representation ensures that the election outcome more accurately reflects people's political wishes.
- ‣ <u>The (vast) majority of</u> fat digestion and absorption occurs in the ileum.
- ‣ This particular gene is expressed <u>predominantly</u> in females.
- ‣ In a civil case the person bringing the lawsuit must produce a <u>preponderance</u> of evidence in their favour.
- ‣ The government's strategy has been only <u>partially</u> successful.
- ‣ Class A drug users represent only <u>a (small) minority of</u> people who use drugs.
- ‣ According to government statistics, sixty-three <u>per cent of</u> girls achieved five or more GCSEs last year.
- ‣ Hong and Slatick (1994) show that only a small <u>percentage</u> of carbon in coal is not oxidised on burning.
- ‣ <u>Of the</u> 85 students, <u>just under // over</u> a third <u>// a half // a quarter</u> said they were unhappy.
- ‣ <u>The top</u> 10 per cent scored 20 <u>or above</u>, and <u>the bottom</u> 10 per cent scored 5 <u>or below</u>.
- ‣ The <u>ratio of</u> women to men in the UK <u>is</u> roughly 1:9

Distribution

The table presents the spatial and temporal <u>distribution of</u> major tremors along the fault line.
The data show an <u>even / uniform // uneven</u> distribution.

10.2 Information to help you use these words correctly

amount n	*Gr* *Amount* is singular and used only with uncountable nouns (compare this with *number of* below). E.g. There **are** a large amount of **studies.** ✗ There **is** a large amount of **research.** ✓
appreciable adj	= A noticeable or significant amount or degree.

approximate adj **approximately** adv	= adj – Almost (but not) exact.
	≠ *Approximately, roughly* and *generally* *Approximately* and *roughly* have similar meanings, but *roughly* is more informal. *Generally* means 'most of the time' or 'in most cases' and should not be used to refer to numerical values or amounts. (See also section 27, page 183.)
capacity n	= The maximum amount something can contain or produce. For the difference between *capacity, ability* and *capability* see section 28, page 191.
degree n	= (1) A unit of measurement for temperature and angle.
	= (2) The extent, size or level of things connected to quality, feelings or impact. E.g. The components were produced to **a high degree** of accuracy. To **a large degree / a large extent**, most people are not interested in political action. (3) An educational award.
	✐ To a **high // large // great / considerable // remarkable // surprising // small // limited** degree.
dimension n	= (1) The scope or physical measurements of something. (2) An aspect or part of something. E.g. The debate has a strong educational dimension.
	✐ An **added / additional // different // extra // further // new** dimension. A **political // social // educational** dimension.
few det / pron	= A small number of.
	Gr *Few* emphasises the fact that there is only a small number or not enough of something. E.g. This is important research as there are few previous studies in this area. *A few* emphasises the positive fact that there are some, although not very many. E.g. There are a few tickets left for the game next week. However, *a few* is informal so in academic writing use *some / a small number of*. E.g. A small number of studies have already been conducted but this one looks at the problem in a new way.

level n / v	= n – (1) An amount. E.g. A high level, the maximum level, at its lowest level. Similar to meaning (2) of *degree* above. (2) A particular standard or status. E.g. **At** a national level, to study **at** university level. (3) A way of understanding something. E.g. This idea can be understood **on** two levels.
maximise v	= To make as big or as good as possible.
	ℰ To maximise **profits** // **gains** // **chances** // **the likelihood of** // **efficiency** // **performance** // **potential** // **productivity**.
maximum adj	= The biggest, greatest or highest amount possible.
minimal adj	= Very small and/or as small as possible.
minimise v	= To make as small, few or low as possible.
	ℰ To minimise the **amount of** // **cost of** // **need for** // **number of** // **danger** // **threat** // **risk** // **damage** // **delay** // **errors** // **impact** // **effect**.
minimum adj	= The smallest, least or lowest possible. E.g. Minimum age, minimum speed.
number of adj / det	= (1) Several / some. (2) The numerical value.
	Gr *Number of* is used only with countable nouns (compare with *amount of* above). E.g. There **is** a large **number of research. ✗** There **are** a large **number of studies. ✓** Definition (1) needs *a* + plural subject and verb. E.g. **A number of** factors **are** problematic. Definition (2) needs *the* + singular third person subject and verb. E.g. **The** high **number of** students **is** a problem.
numerous adj	= Many.
	Gr *Numerous* is used only with plural, countable nouns. E.g. There **is numerous research** in this area. ✗ There **are numerous** research in this area. ✗ There **are numerous** research **studies** in this area. ✓

partially adv **partial** adj	= adv – Not completely / only to some extent. E.g. I am partially blind. The project was partially successful. adj – (1) Incomplete or only in parts. (2) Biased. (3) 'Having a liking for'. ≠ *Partially* and *partly* These words can often be used interchangeably (although *partially* is more formal) but there is a degree of difference in meaning. *Partially* emphasises that something has not happened to completion, whereas *partly* emphasises the idea of different parts or elements. E.g. The house is built partly of concrete and partly of wood. For *impartial* see section 19, page 121.
per cent n **percentage** n	*Gr* Use *per cent* when you include the actual number (e.g. 15 per cent) and *percentage* when you don't. ✳ *Per cent* is the British spelling and *percent* is the common spelling in the US.
preponderance n	= Superiority in power, importance or amount.
profound adj **profundity** n	= adj – Very great, deep and/or significant. ⌀ A profound **effect** / **impact** // **consequence** // **implication** // **influence**, profound **repercussions**. Profound **shock** // **sadness**. A profound **change** // **shift** // **transformation** // **problem** // **understanding** // **knowledge**.
pronounced adj	= Very noticeable.
proportion n	= A share or number of something in relation to the whole. ≠ X is **in** // **out of** proportion to Y. We need to keep **a sense of** proportion.

proportional adj **proportionality** n	=	adj – Corresponding in size and/or ratio. In mathematics, *proportional* and *proportionality* have the more precise meaning of two things that always increase and/or decrease by a constant ratio.
	≠	*Proportionality* and *correlation* *Correlation* is only used in the context of statistics, and does not involve a constant ration of increase or decrease.
proportionate adj	=	Corresponding or appropriate to the amount, size or quality of something else.
	≠	*Proportionate* and *proportional* Although these words can be used interchangeably, they do have a small difference in meaning. As shown by the definitions, *proportionate* tends to be used when the related items are of different natures and not directly measurable. E.g. The type of homework given should be proportionate to the age of the child.
quantify v	=	v – To measure the amount of something.
quantifiable adj	=	adj – Capable of being measured.

10.3 Nearly but not quite right

The sentences on the left contain the types of mistakes people make when using words from this section. The correct versions are given on the right.

	Incorrect	Correct
1	Evidence shows that a significant <u>amount of</u> teenagers have tried drugs.	Evidence shows that a significant <u>number of</u> teenagers have tried drugs.
2	The UK population is <u>generally</u> 61 million.	The UK population is <u>approximately</u> 61 million.
3	Enormous amounts of pressure <u>was</u> applied onto the heart.	Enormous amounts of pressure <u>were</u> applied onto the heart.
4	Twelve per cent of people in the study <u>is</u> from mixed ethnic backgrounds.	Twelve per cent of people in the study <u>are</u> from mixed ethnic backgrounds.

	Incorrect	Correct
5	There is a <u>large</u> possibility that the experiment was flawed.	There is a <u>strong</u> possibility that the experiment was flawed.
6	The population rose by three <u>percentage</u> a year.	The population rose by three <u>per cent</u> a year.
7	Someone contemplating suicide may feel that there are <u>a few</u> reasons to continue living.	Someone contemplating suicide may feel that there are <u>few</u> reasons to continue living.
8	This debate can be interpreted <u>in</u> two levels.	This debate can be interpreted <u>on</u> two levels.
9	The company's wireless security needs to be set <u>to the strongest</u> level.	The company's wireless security needs to be set <u>to the highest</u> level.
10	The <u>degrees for</u> job satisfaction <u>have</u> an impact on general happiness.	The <u>degree of / level of</u> job satisfaction <u>has</u> an impact on general happiness.

Movement and change, getting better or worse, allowing or preventing and eliminating

● ● ● ● ● ●

11   Movement, change, trend and tendency

11.1   Words in action

Increase and decrease

‣ The global population <u>increased / rose</u> dramatically in the nineteenth century.
‣ Irish GDP <u>fell / decreased</u> in the first quarter of the year.
‣ The regime's power has <u>diminished / lessened</u> in recent months.
‣ Cardioinhibitory drugs <u>reduce</u> heart rate.
‣ The rate of new cases <u>reached a peak</u> // <u>hit a low</u> in August.

Amount of increase or decrease

‣ The graph shows a ⌉ <u>minimal / negligible</u>   ⌉ <u>rise / increase</u>.
                       <u>small / slight</u>   <u>decline / decrease / fall / drop</u>.
                       <u>marked / significant / substantial / noticeable</u>   <u>dip</u>.
                    ⌋ <u>pronounced</u>   ⌋ <u>fluctuation</u>.

‣ Prices <u>rose</u> // <u>fell</u> <u>slightly</u> // <u>noticeably</u> // <u>markedly / significantly</u>.

Speed or rate of increase or decrease

‣ The graph shows a   ⌉ <u>gradual</u>
                                   <u>steady</u>   ⌉ <u>rise / increase</u>.
                                ⌋ <u>dramatic / sharp / sudden</u>   <u>decline / decrease / fall / drop</u>.
The graph shows that there was a   <u>dramatic / sharp / sudden</u>   <u>fluctuation</u>.
                                                             ⌋ <u>dip</u>.

‣ Prices <u>rose</u> // <u>fell</u> <u>gradually</u> // <u>steadily</u> // <u>sharply</u> // <u>suddenly</u> // <u>dramatically</u>.
‣ The new drug has been shown to <u>accelerate</u> // <u>decelerate</u> the healing of burn injuries.
‣ The <u>rate of</u> change over the month was greater than expected.
‣ Research shows that the rate of so-called 'child crime' has increased <u>exponentially</u> over the last decade.

Changeability and instability

▸ The political boundaries of the region are extremely <u>changeable / mutable.</u>
▸ The computer software is <u>flexible / versatile / adaptable</u> enough to cope with all gaming platforms.
▸ General relativity predicts that the universe is either <u>contracting</u> or <u>expanding</u>.
▸ The financial market is in <u>(a state of) flux</u> due to the uncertainty surrounding the election.
▸ Mutual funds cause short-term <u>volatility / instability</u> in credit markets.

Stability and lack of movement

▸ The population of New Zealand's rarest seabird has <u>retained / kept</u> a good level of genetic diversity.
▸ Our results suggest that student numbers will <u>level off / level out / reach a plateau</u> over the next few years.
▸ Rates of infection <u>stabilised / became stable</u> once a hand-washing regime had been established.
▸ The economy has <u>remained stable</u> over the last twelve months.
▸ Sales have <u>remained</u> <u>static / fixed / stationary</u> over the last three years.

Accumulation and growth

▸ Salt-tolerant plants <u>accumulate</u> salt in their leaves rather than their fruit.
▸ Repetitive strain injury (RSI) is a form of <u>cumulative</u> trauma disorder.
▸ The <u>proliferation of / expansion of / growth of / increase in</u> mutual funds <u>adds to</u> market instability.

Trend and projection

▸ Figure 1 shows <u>an upward trend // a downward trend</u> in male suicides.
▸ The study highlights a worrying <u>trend towards / trend of</u> women fearing to walk alone at night.
▸ Global temperatures are <u>projected // predicted</u> to <u>rise // fall</u> by 1 to 3 degrees over the next twenty years.

Tendency

▸ Sleep-deprived nurses <u>have a greater</u> <u>tendency to / propensity to</u> eat junk food than …
▸ Sleep-deprived nurses <u>are more likely to / are more inclined to</u> make medical errors than …

Change and transition

▸ There has been little <u>change / alteration</u> to the current legislation.
▸ These plants have been genetically <u>altered</u> so that they have a longer shelf life.
▸ The research team <u>modified / adapted / adjusted</u> its procedures to give more time for sample analysis.

- The management <u>restructuring</u> of the university has helped to reduce salary costs.
- The protest helped to bring about a <u>shift</u> in the government's position on the issue.
- Olson et al. (2001) present a model for seamless <u>transition</u> from student to Registered Nurse.
- The invention of the printing press <u>transformed</u> European society.
- The announcement represents <u>a radical change in</u> tax policy / <u>a radical departure from</u> previous tax policy.
- Impressionism <u>evolved</u> from the naturalist and realist schools.

11.2 Information to help you use these words correctly

accumulate v **accumulative** adj	= v – To build up or increase slowly over time. 🖌 v – To accumulate **assets** // **capital** // **profit** // **interest** // **wealth** // **debt** // **evidence** // **knowledge** // **skill**. ✳ The adjective is *accumulative* but the synonym *cumulative* is now more commonly used. E.g. The return on the investment is cumulative.
adapt v **adaptable** adj	= v – To change (or change something) in order to fit a new or different purpose, or to deal with a new situation. Similar to meaning (1) of *adjust*, below. 🖌 To **easily / readily / quickly // successfully** adapt. **To find it difficult to** adapt. **To** adapt **well to** X. To adapt X **to** Y. To adapt to **change** // **the environment** // **circumstance** // **a lifestyle** / **a way of life** // **a situation** // **surroundings**.
adjust v **adjustable** adj	= v – (1) To change (or change something) in order to fit a new or different purpose or to deal with a new situation. Similar to *adapt*. (2) In relation to position, temperature etc. to alter slightly in order to better fit the desired purpose or user.
alter v	= To change, usually in a small but significant way. Similar to *modify*.

diminish v	= (1) To make less or appear to make less. (2) To take away from something's / someone's power, authority or reputation. *∂* To diminish in **strength** // **size** // **power** // **authority** // **importance** / **significance** // **popularity** // **credibility**. The **capacity** // **resource** // **supply** // **number** // **impact** // **risk** // **threat** // **likelihood** // **chance of** Y has diminished. The **light** / **pain** diminishes. To diminish **the appearance of** X.
evolve v	= To develop gradually. Sometimes used to describe development from something simple to something more complex. *Gr* To evolve **from** X **into** Y.
expand v **expandable** adj	= v – To increase, spread or to give further details about something. adj – Able to expand. *≠* *Expandable* and *expendable* *Expendable* means not important and easily done without. E.g. Managers should value employees rather than think of them as expendable.
exponentially adv **exponential** adj **exponent** n	= adv – At an increasingly rapid rate. adj – Increasingly rapid. E.g. Exponential growth. n – Someone who actively supports or exemplifies something. (See section 19, page 120.) *＊* *Exponent*, *exponential* and *exponentially* have more specialised meanings in mathematics.
flux n	= In a state of change. In science, *flux* has the specific meaning of the rate at which energy or matter flows.
incline v **inclination** n	= v – (1) To want or tend to do something. (2) To lean or be at an angle. *Gr* v – **To be inclined to do** something. E.g. People are inclined to act aggressively when under severe stress. n – To **have** / **feel** / **show** an inclination to do X.

lessen v	= To decrease or reduce.
	🖉 To lessen the **likelihood** // **chance** // **risk** // **effect** // **impact** // **chance** // **disruption** // **burden** // **pain** // **suffering** // **stress** // **tension** (of X).
modify v **modification** n	= v – To make small alterations to something specific, such as a particular process, physical structure or document. Similar to *alter*.
mutable adj	= Capable of change.
proliferation n	= An increase in the number of something and/or the spread of something. Often used to describe a sudden increase or spread.
propensity n	= A tendency / inclination.
	𝒢𝓇 A propensity **for + noun** (e.g. aggression) / A propensity + **infinitive** (e.g. to act aggressively).
radical adj / n **radically** adv	= adj – (1) Fundamental and/or large. (2) Extreme, very different from the norm. (See section 19, page 122.) (3) Promoting fundamental political and social change.
	🖉 A radical **shift** // **transformation** // **change** // **improvement** // **restructuring** // **reform**.
rate n / v	= n – (1) A measure, quantity or frequency measured against something else, usually time. (2) A measured quantity or proportion. E.g. Interest rate, death rate, growth rate. v – To give a value or ranking according to a particular scale.
reduce v **reduction** n	= v – (1) To decrease, bring down or lower the level, size, amount or power of something. (2) To break something down to its fundamental elements for the purpose of analysis.
	🖉 To reduce X **to** Y. To reduce X **in** Y. To reduce X **to the level of** Y.
retain v	= To continue to have or keep possession of.

rise v / n	*Gr* The past tense of *rise* is *rose*. E.g. Prices rose last year. The present perfect form is *risen*. E.g. Prices have risen since last year. ≠ *Rise, raise* and *arise* To *rise* means to increase, go up or get up. It uses <u>a subject</u> but **no object**. E.g. <u>Prices</u> rise **goods** when demand is high. ✗ <u>Prices</u> rise when demand is high. ✓ To *raise* means to lift, promote or bring up. Raise needs both a <u>subject</u> and **an object**. E.g. <u>The government</u> will raise in an attempt to deter heavy drinking. ✗ <u>The government</u> will raise **tax on alcohol** in an attempt to deter heavy drinking. ✓ **Taxes** have been raised <u>(by the government)</u>. ✓ To *arise* means to come into existence / originate. *Arise* is usually used when a problem, issue or situation first develops. E.g. The issue arose at the meeting yesterday. Another meaning of *arise* is to get up (similar to *rise*) but this is no longer common usage.
shift n / v	= n – A significant change or move. *ℰ* A **radical** // **fundamental** // **rapid** / **sudden** shift (in X). A shift in **position** / **stance** // **emphasis** // **focus** // **attention** // **debate** // **discussion** // **perception** // **perspective**.
stable adj **stabilise** n	= adj – Not changing, not likely to change, or having only small changes. *ℰ* Stable **economy** // **value** // **inflation** // **rate** // **price** // **situation** // **ground** // **platform** // **personality** // **household** // **family** // **population**. ✳ Usually used with the positive association of the stability being desired, calm and/or supportive. (Compare with *static* below.)
static adj	= Lacking any movement. Sometimes used with negative associations of being unable to move or change.

tendency n tend v	=	n – (1) A characteristic or behaviour that occurs quite often or is likely to happen. (2) An inclination towards a particular behaviour.
	Gr	A tendency **to do** X. X **tends to do** Y.
	&#x1F58B;	A **clear** // **marked** / **pronounced** / **strong** // **slight** // **worrying** tendency. A **natural** // **violent** // **aggressive** // **inherent** // **instinctive** tendency. To **have** // **display** // **exhibit** // **show** // **indicate** // **reveal** // **suggest** // **reinforce** // **avoid** // **resist** a tendency.
transformation n transform v	=	n – A fundamental and/or complete change. v – To change fundamentally and/or completely.
transition n transitional adj	=	n – The process of changing or adapting to a new situation or position.
	&#x1F58B;	**To make** a transition. **To undergo** a transition. A **seamless** / **smooth** / **easy** // **successful** // **painful** // **difficult** // **gradual** // **sudden** transition.
trend n	=	(1) A general direction of movement. E.g. A downward trend in house sales. (2) A particular fashion.
	&#x1F58B;	An **upward** // **downward** // **emerging** // **current** // **prevailing** // **long-term** // **short-term** // **worrying** // **significant** // **general** // **underlying** // **national** // **global** trend.
versatile adj	=	(1) Able to adapt or be adapted for different functions or purposes. Similar to *adaptable*. (2) (Of people) Having several or many different skills.
volatile adj	=	Unstable, liable to change quickly.

11.3 Nearly but not quite right

The sentences on the left contain the types of mistakes people make when using words from this section. The correct versions are given on the right.

	Incorrect	Correct
1	They are both <u>at a state of</u> balance.	They are both <u>in a state of</u> balance.

	Incorrect	Correct
2	The issue that <u>arises to</u> many consumers is lack of accountability.	The issue that <u>arises for</u> many consumers is lack of accountability.
3	<u>Bird flu could elevate to a higher risk</u> if precautions are not taken.	<u>The risk of bird flu could</u> <u>increase / rise</u> if precautions are not taken.
4	There was <u>a raise</u> in 2005 followed by a slight dip in 2006.	There was <u>a rise</u> in 2005 followed by a slight dip in 2006.
5	Profits have been rising <u>highly</u>.	Profits have been rising <u>sharply / steeply / suddenly / dramatically</u>.
6	The chancellor suggested substantial <u>modifications</u> to all areas of spending.	The chancellor suggested substantial <u>changes</u> to all areas of spending.
7	The <u>transformation</u> from school to university can be difficult.	The <u>transition</u> from school to university can be difficult.
8	Hirsch et al. (2001) assert that universities are <u>at a state of flux</u>.	Hirsch et al. (2001) assert that universities are <u>in a state of flux</u>.
9	Since 2010 the number of cases has <u>raised</u>.	Since 2010 the number of cases has <u>risen</u>.
10	Deforestation <u>enhances the level of greenhouse gases</u>.	Deforestation <u>increases the level of greenhouse gases</u>.

12 Getting better or worse, bringing back or taking away, encouraging or deterring

12.1 Words in action

Getting better, easier or bringing back

- The medicine will <u>relieve</u> the symptoms.
- The IMF loan <u>eased / alleviated / ameliorated</u> the country's financial problems.
- Owens et al. (1992) look at whether physical activity can <u>mitigate</u> the effects of aging.
- Meta-cognitive theory <u>enhances / expands / improves / helps / facilitates</u> our understanding of stress.
- The constitutional reforms helped to <u>restore</u> the balance of power.
- Liquid intake <u>compensates for</u> fluid loss in the body.
- Gandhi's principle of non-cooperation helped Indians <u>regain</u> a sense of national identity.
- There has been <u>a resurgence of</u> human tuberculosis in the UK.

Getting worse, harder or taking away

- The study suggests that depression <u>aggravates / exacerbates / worsens</u> inflammatory disease.
- Social cohesion in nineteenth-century London <u>deteriorated</u> as a direct result of the high mortality rate.
- I will argue that continuous assessment can <u>detract from</u> student learning.
- Being excluded from the workforce can <u>erode // undermine</u> self-confidence.
- In the second test the questions were <u>more difficult / harder</u> to answer.

Encouraging

- Cunningham (2011) asks why governments <u>make concessions to</u> some protest groups but not others.
- RIBA educational boards <u>encourage / foster</u> innovation in how architecture is taught.
- I argue that international charities <u>reinforce</u> negative stereotypes of Africa.
- We suggest that certain TV programmes <u>perpetuate</u> a north–south divide in the UK.

Deterring

- The negotiations were successful in <u>deterring</u> further conflict.
- Lack of stimulation in infancy has been shown to <u>hinder / impede</u> later intellectual development.
- The new policing policy has successfully <u>curtailed / reduced</u> violent crime.
- The government claims that the opposition tried to <u>interfere with / disrupt</u> the referendum.
- The chemical <u>inhibits / restricts / curtails / limits</u> plant growth.

12.2   Information to help you use these words correctly

aggravate v	= (1) To make worse. (2) To annoy. (This is a more informal meaning of *aggravate*, not usually used in academic study.) ✐ To aggravate a **condition** // **illness** // **symptom** // **problem**.
alleviate v	= To make less painful, harmful or difficult. Often used in the context of illness. ✐ To alleviate **pain** // **symptoms** // **anxiety** // **pressure** // **depression** // **hardship** // **poverty** // **hunger** // **the problem**.
ameliorate v	= To make better and/or to improve a painful, harmful or difficult situation.
compensate v **compensatory** adj	= v – To do or give something that makes up for a loss, reduction, bad effect or injury.
concession n **concede** v	= n – A bargain or compromise. v – To finally or grudgingly admit the truth or existence of something. E.g. The newspaper maintained the truth of the article but conceded that it might have upset some people. (See also section 19, page 119, and section 26 introduction, page 173.)
curtail v	= To restrict or limit, often via the use of force or legislation. ✐ To curtail **freedom** // **growth** // **spending** // **inflation** // **crime**.
deter v **deterrent** n	= v – To discourage, to make something unlikely or to prevent. (See also section 13, page 81.)
deteriorate v	= To get progressively worse.
detract v	= To make something less beneficial or good. Gr The detailed statistical data in the report **detracts from** the main findings. ≠ *Detract* and *distract* To *distract* means to take someone's attention away from something. Similar to *divert*. (See section 25, page 167.)

enhance v	= To increase the quality, value or extent of something positive.
	ℰ To **chemically** // **artificially** // **digitally** enhance something. To enhance **credibility** // **production** // **competitiveness** // **performance** // **knowledge** // **skills** // **understanding** // **experience** // **knowledge**.
erode v	= To decrease or wear away gradually.
	ℰ To erode **trust** // **support** // **confidence** // **value**.
exacerbate v	= To make a situation, pain or feeling worse. Similar to *worsen* and *aggravate*.
	ℰ To exacerbate a/the **situation** // **problem** // **symptom** // **cough** // **headache**.
facilitate v **facility** n	= v – To help, make easier or to make possible. n – *Facility* usually refers to a building or service. E.g. The university has state of the art facilities. However, *facility* can also be used to mean 'natural talent'. E.g. I have a facility for learning languages.
foster v	= To encourage, nurture or develop something.
	ℰ To foster **collaboration** // **cooperation** // **partnership** // **relations** // **growth** // **development** // **learning** // **creativity**.
hinder v **hindrance** n	= v – To delay, obstruct or prevent. Similar to *impede* and *inhibit*.
	ℰ To hinder **an attempt** // **development** // **growth** // **progress** // **performance** // **movement** // **communication** // **understanding** // **attempt** // **recovery**.
impede v	= To delay, obstruct or prevent. Similar to *hinder* and *inhibit*.
inhibit v **inhibitor** n **inhibitive/ory** adj	= v – To hinder, restrict or prevent a process, action or behaviour. n – A substance that slows down or prevents a (chemical) process. E.g. An enzyme inhibitor binds to the enzyme, thereby decreasing or preventing its activity.

mitigate v **mitigation** n	= v – To make something less harmful, painful or serious. E.g. The food aid helped to mitigate the effects of the famine. ≠ *Mitigate* and *militate* *To militate* is to have a powerful effect against, or to cast doubt on something. E.g. The evidence militates against his innocence.
perpetuate v	= To cause a situation to continue. Often (but not always) used for negative things. 𝒫 To perpetuate (a/n) **idea** // **belief** // **lie** // **myth** // **stereotype** // **inequality** // **injustice** // **violence** // **cycle**.
regain v	= To get back something that was lost. E.g. The elected government regained power with the help of the rebel soldiers. 𝒫 To regain **respect** // **confidence** // **credibility** // **fitness** // **strength** // **dignity** // **control** // **power** // // **sovereignty** // **independence**.
relieve v	= To decrease or remove something harmful or painful. Similar to *alleviate*. 𝒫 To relieve **pain** // **symptoms** // **anxiety** // **boredom** // **suffering** // **poverty**.
restore v	= To cause a situation or practice to exist again. E.g. The rebel soldiers helped restore power to the elected government. 𝒫 To restore **confidence** // **power** // **democracy** // **order** // **stability** // **discipline** // **normality** // **harmony** // **balance** // **peace** // **faith** // **pride**.
resurgence n	= The (often rapid) return of something that had previously declined or disappeared.
undermine v	= To cause something to become less confident, successful or powerful.

12.3   Nearly but not quite right

The sentences on the left contain the types of mistakes people make when using words from this section. The correct versions are given on the right.

	Incorrect	Correct
1	Eating more carrots will <u>restore</u> the symptoms of vitamin A deficiency.	Eating more carrots will <u>relieve / alleviate</u> the symptoms of vitamin A deficiency.
2	The legislation is unlikely <u>to alleviate the issue</u>.	The legislation is unlikely <u>to resolve the issue</u>.
3	There has been a <u>resurgence in</u> nationalism in the region.	There has been a <u>resurgence of</u> nationalism in the region.
4	Mixing the two drugs will <u>enhance</u> the risk of damage.	Mixing the two drugs will <u>increase</u> the risk of damage.
5	Pollution from factories in China has <u>exaggerated</u> global warming.	Pollution from factories in China has <u>exacerbated</u> global warming.
6	The studies <u>ameliorate</u> our knowledge of sub-atomic particles.	The studies <u>enhance / expand / increase / improve / facilitate</u> our knowledge of sub-atomic particles.
7	The new legislation will foster <u>employing</u> immigrants.	The new legislation will foster <u>(the) employment of</u> immigrants.
8	Poor management gradually <u>deterred</u> morale within the organisation.	Poor management gradually <u>undermined / eroded</u> morale within the organisation.
9	The many detailed references <u>subtract</u> from the clarity of the report.	The many detailed references <u>detract</u> from the clarity of the report.
10	Rush et al. (2004) investigate alternative treatments to <u>relief</u> major depression.	Rush et al. (2004) investigate alternative treatments to <u>relieve</u> major depression.

13   Allowing or preventing, avoiding, excluding, cancelling out and eliminating

13.1   Words in action

Allowing

▸ The method we used <u>permitted / allowed / enabled</u> us to analyse each sound separately.

Deterring and preventing

▸ I argue that the death penalty does not <u>deter</u> serious crime.
▸ Oscar Wilde's maternal in-laws tried to <u>prevent</u> him from seeing his children.
▸ Condensation on the inside surface of lenses can <u>obstruct / block</u> vision.
▸ The protesters claimed they were <u>denied</u> access to legal representation.
▸ The cost of making a house fully energy-efficient can be <u>prohibitive</u>.

Avoiding or the unavoidable

▸ Using synonyms is one way of <u>avoiding</u> repetition.
▸ Assunta (2004) looks at how tobacco companies <u>circumvented</u> Singapore's ban on cigarette advertising.
▸ Some business costs, such as sunk costs, are <u>unavoidable</u>.
▸ It is incorrect to associate aging with an <u>inexorable</u> decline in muscle mass.
▸ A funding decrease next year seems <u>inevitable</u>.

Excluding and keeping separate

▸ We found that openly homosexual employees were regularly <u>excluded from</u> senior management posts.
▸ <u>The exclusion of</u> women from the national team was questioned in parliament.
▸ This case study looks at protective legislation for <u>marginalised</u> indigenous communities in Nepal.
▸ The Jim Crow laws, legitimising racial <u>segregation</u> in the US Southern states, were in place until 1965.

Cancelling out or eliminating

▸ The drug has proved successful in <u>counteracting / negating / nullifying</u> the effects of the virus.
▸ One aim of the government report is to <u>dispel</u> rumours of divisions within the party.
▸ Human tuberculosis had not been <u>eradicated / eliminated</u> in Britain.
▸ Translation technology may one day <u>obviate / eliminate</u> the need for learning foreign languages.

13.2 Information to help you use these words correctly

circumvent v	=	To get round something, obtaining your goal by a different means. Often used in the context of regulations and laws.
counteract v	=	To act against something in order to cancel out or reduce the effect or force of something else. E.g. The website gives advice on how to counteract the effects of caffeine. For *counterpart* see section 21, page 138 and for *to counter* see section 23, page 153.
deter v **deterrent** n	=	v – To discourage. To make something unlikely, or to prevent.
	Gr	Deter + noun. E.g. The death penalty does not deter **crime**. Deter + object + from + verb -ing. E.g. The death penalty does not **deter people from** commit**ting** crimes.
dispel v	=	To make a rumour, belief, feeling, doubt or idea cease to exist.
	≠	*Dispel*, *expel* and *disperse* *To expel* means to drive out by force. *To disperse* means to scatter or spread over a wide area. (See section 14, page 86.)
eradicate v	=	To destroy completely. Similar to *eliminate*.
	✍	To eradicate **completely // systematically // effectively // permanently // successfully**. To eradicate **hunger // poverty // disease // a pest**.
inevitable adj	=	Certain to happen. *Inevitable* is used to describe an unavoidable event or end result of a process.
inexorable adj	=	Impossible to prevent or stop. *Inexorable* is used to describe an unavoidable 'slowly but surely' process that has a pre-determined end result.

marginalise v marginalisation n marginal adj	= v – To treat as unimportant and/or as of low status, or to exclude. (See also section 21, page 140.)
	Gr Often used in the passive. E.g. The group was marginalised because of its religion.
negate v **negation** n	= v – To completely cancel out the effect of something. Similar to *nullify*.
nullify v	= To completely cancel out the effect of something. Similar to *negate*.
obviate v	= (1) To remove the need for something. E.g. Mobile networks obviate the need for wired services. (2) To prevent or avoid. E.g. This installation method obviates mechanical stress.
	⊘ To obviate **the need for** X.
permit v / n	= v – (1) To enable. Similar to *allow*. E.g. The results permit us to draw the conclusion that … (2) To give permission.
	✳ The verb is pronounced per<u>mit</u> and the noun is pronounced <u>per</u>mit.
segregation n **segregate** v	= n – Forced separation from other groups.
	⊘ **Racial // gender // ethnic // social // religious** segregation. To **fight // resist // challenge // encourage // enforce // ensure // maintain // promote** segregation. v – To segregate X **from** Y.

13.3 Nearly but not quite right

The sentences on the left contain the types of mistakes people make when using words from this section. The correct versions are given on the right.

	Incorrect	Correct
1	The army used tear gas to <u>dispel</u> the demonstrators.	The army used tear gas to <u>disperse</u> the demonstrators.

	Incorrect	Correct
2	The state government has brought in changes that people are allowed to carry guns.	The state government has brought in changes that allow / enable people to carry guns.
3	Philip Morris and other companies avoided Singapore's advertising laws and promoted their products successfully.	Philip Morris and other companies circumvented Singapore's advertising laws and promoted their products successfully.
4	The act allows that any person below the income threshold can have free legal aid.	The act allows / enables / permits any person below the income threshold to have free legal aid.
5	The report claims that an 8–10% increase in energy efficiency will obviate new power plants.	The report claims that an 8–10% increase in energy efficiency will obviate the need for new power plants.
6	I suggest that the new curriculum will lead to religious education in schools being marginal.	I suggest that the curriculum will lead to religious education in schools being marginalised.
7	This tubule lets the blood take out waste from the blood.	This tubule allows / enables the blood to take out waste from the blood.
8	Christian groups are concerned about the excluding of religious education from the list of core subjects.	Christian groups are concerned about the exclusion of religious education from the list of core subjects.
9	Dartnell believes it is inexorable that humans will one day colonise other planets.	Dartnell believes it is inevitable that humans will one day colonise other planets.
10	The pill counter acts the effects of alcohol.	The pill counteracts / counters the effects of alcohol.

Circumstance, advantage or disadvantage, presence or absence, and importance

● ● ● ● ● ●

14 Circumstance, occurrence, normality, norm, deviance, risk, and threat

See also section 7 (time and sequence), section 15 (advantages and disadvantages) and section 16 (importance and influence) for other relevant words and phrases.

14.1 Words in action

Circumstance and situation

▸ During the Great Depression, <u>circumstances were such that</u> civil unrest became common.
▸ By the end of the century, the <u>circumstances</u> were <u>favourable</u> // <u>advantageous</u> // <u>positive</u>.
▸ The political <u>situation is (highly) complex</u> // <u>(relatively) straightforward</u>.
▸ The <u>adverse</u> // <u>hostile</u> situation that existed within the company contributed to its liquidation.

Occurrence and events

▸ The study looks at <u>the occurrence of</u> eye movement during sleep.
▸ The report outlines how lifestyle interventions can reduce the <u>incidence</u> of type 2 diabetes.
▸ Photosynthesis is a natural <u>phenomenon</u> in all plants.
▸ The signing of the Treaty of Tlatelolco was an important <u>event</u> for Latin America.
▸ Any <u>incident</u> of racism in the workplace should be taken seriously by management.

Commonness and distribution

▸ The practice of horizontal oil drilling is becoming increasingly <u>common</u>.
  Research has revealed <u>widespread</u> misunderstanding about the causes of arthritis.
▸ I will argue that <u>systemic</u> racism in the police force no longer exists.

- Poverty is often <u>concentrated in</u> neighbourhoods rather than <u>spread</u> (<u>uniformly / in a uniform way</u>) across a city.
- Australia has a <u>sparse</u> population overall but relatively <u>dense</u> pockets of urban habitation.
- Virtual conferencing is a boon for geographically <u>dispersed</u> organisations.
- The food industry has argued that <u>the prevalence of</u> obesity is due mainly to lifestyle choices.
- There is a <u>pervasive</u> sense of loneliness throughout the novel.
- A lack of women working in science <u>persists</u>, despite government initiatives.

Normality, norms, conformity and deviance

- It is <u>normal</u> business practice for a company to have external auditors.
- The UN delegation asked local leaders to help restore <u>normality</u> in the region.
- The study shows that accepted <u>norms</u> of classroom behaviour are influenced by its gender balance.
- In Christianity, the Holy Family represents <u>normative</u> family values.
- The aim of audit committees is to ensure that companies <u>comply with</u> the regulations.
- Hyde argues that the pressure to <u>conform</u> limits adolescents' ability to consider alternative gender identities.
- Abnormal behaviour is that which not only <u>deviates from</u> the norm but which is also undesirable.

Risk and threat

- Stampfer (1993) looked at possible links between vitamin E intake and <u>risk of</u> heart disease.
- This study examines the extent to which <u>threat of</u> takeover affects productivity.
- Huddy et al. (2005) found that those anxious about <u>threats to</u> security were less supportive of military action.
- Hur has shown that teenagers are more <u>vulnerable to / prone to</u> Internet addiction disorder than other age groups.

14.2 Information to help you use these words correctly

adverse adj	= Bad, unpleasant and/or harmful.
	ℰ An adverse **effect** // **side-effect** // **reaction** // **impact** // **situation** // **outcome** / **consequence**. Adverse **publicity** // **conditions**.
	≠ *Adverse* and *averse* To be *averse* to something means to not like or want it, or to be opposed to it. (See section 19, page 119.) E.g. Most investors are fundamentally risk-averse.
circumstance n	= The condition or fact that affects a situation.
	𝒢𝓇 Usually used in the plural. The circumstances **surrounding** X. **Under** difficult circumstances.
	ℰ **Exceptional** // **special** // **normal** // **unusual** // **unforeseen** // **challenging** / **difficult** circumstances.
comply v **compliance** n	= v – To behave according to a rule, regulation, standard or wish in a specific situation.
	𝒢𝓇 To **comply with** X.
conform v **conformity** n	= v – (1) To behave according to generally accepted social patterns or standards. (2) To be similar to an already established type, form or idea. E.g. The restaurant conforms to people's idea of a family business. (See section 9, page 56.)
	𝒢𝓇 To **conform to** X.
dense adj	= Crowded or closely compacted.
disperse v **dispersed** adj **dispersal** n	= v – To go, spread out or break up over a large (or larger) area.
	ℰ v – To disperse **rioters** // **crowds** // **groups** // **demonstrators**. The rioters **were quickly** // **rapidly** // **gradually** dispersed. adj – The tribes are **geographically** // **widely** dispersed.
	≠ *Disperse* and *dispel*. (See section 13, page 81.)

incidence n	= The frequency or number of times something happens.
	✎ A **high** // **average** // **low** // **annual** // **recorded** // **reported** // **estimated** // **actual** incidence. To **increase** // **reduce** the incidence of X. A **fall** // **rise** in the incidence of X.
	≠ *Incidence* and *incident* An *incident* is a specific event, usually one that is negative and/or harmful. *Event* is usually a more appropriate word to use in academic writing.
	✳ The adjective *incidental* and adverb *incidentally* have the different meaning of 'less important' or 'as a by-product of something else'. (See also section 16, page 100.)
natural adj	= Existing in nature, not artificial or man-made.
	✎ A natural **product** // **resource** // **substance** // **consequence** // **reaction** // **phenomenon** // **tendency**.
norm n **normative** adj	= n – The normal, typical or prescribed social behaviour or situation. adj – *Normative* has some additional, more specialised meanings. In academic study, a normative statement is one based on a value judgement rather than fact. E.g. 'Murderers should be given the death penalty' is a normative statement or claim.
	✎ n – The **established** // **expected** // **prevailing** // **traditional** norm. A **cultural** // **social** // **religious** norm.
occurrence n **occur** v	= n – Something that takes place or exists.
	✎ A **daily** // **yearly** // **common** // **regular** // **widespread** // **rare** // **isolated** // **natural** // **normal** // **unexpected** occurrence.
	✳ *Incident, predicament* and *happening* These three words are all usually used in informal, dramatic or literary contexts. The verb *to happen* is also usually too informal for academic writing. E.g. The interviews happened in April. ✗ The interviews took place / occurred in April. ✓

persistent adj **persist** v **persistence** n	= adj – When something or someone refuses to stop, let go or go away. 🖉 A persistent **attack** // **refusal** // **illness** // **failure** // **belief** // **myth** // **misconception** // **misunderstanding**.
pervasive adj	= Widespread and dominant. 🖉 A pervasive **influence** // **attitude** // **presence** // **problem** // **belief**.
prevalent adj **prevalence** n	= adj – Common and/or dominant, often within a small area or at a particular point in time. 𝒢𝓇 n – **The** prevalence **of** X.
risk n / v	= n – Having the potential to be harmful, dangerous or unpleasant. v – To expose to harm or danger. ✳ The adjective *risky* is usually too informal for academic writing.
sparse adj	= Distributed thinly and/or existing in only small amounts.
systemic adj	= Relating to, or spread throughout, a whole system or organism. 🖉 A systemic **disease** // **effect** // **risk** // **problem** // **failure**. ≠ *Systemic* and *systematic* *Systematic* means 'according to a particular system, method or plan' as in a systematic approach, classification, course. (See also section 8, page 53.)
vulnerable adj	= Exposed to, or likely to be harmed or attacked, either mentally or physically. 🖉 **Highly** // **particularly** // **increasingly** // **emotionally** // **mentally** // **physically** // **economically** // **financially** vulnerable. To **be** // **appear** // **seem** // **feel** vulnerable **to** X.
widespread adj	= Spread over a large area. 🖉 A widespread **occurrence** // **phenomenon** // **assumption** // **belief** // **perception** // **misconception**. Widespread **speculation** // **consultation** // **concern** // **criticism** // **ignorance** // **misunderstanding** // **corruption** // **disease** // **deprivation** // **suffering** // **poverty** // **unemployment**.

14.3 Nearly but not quite right

The sentences on the left contain the types of mistakes people make when using words from this section. The correct versions are given on the right.

	Incorrect	Correct
1	Poverty is one of the major <u>occurrences affecting the world</u>.	Poverty is one of the world's major <u>problems.</u>
2	Discrimination can <u>be through many ways</u>.	Discrimination can <u>occur in many ways / manifest itself in many ways</u>.
3	'Relative poverty' is a term that <u>comes up a lot</u> in the world today.	'Relative poverty' is a <u>prevalent term / much used term.</u>
4	Tourism <u>causes</u> many environmental <u>threats</u>.	Tourism <u>poses</u> many environmental <u>threats</u>.
5	A weak immune system leaves the person more vulnerable <u>in</u> infection.	A weak immune system leaves the person more vulnerable <u>to</u> infection.
6	Discrimination occurs <u>across</u> many jobs.	Discrimination occurs <u>in</u> many jobs.
7	I will argue that the Wuchang uprising is the most important <u>incident</u> in modern Chinese history.	I will argue that the Wuchang uprising is the most important <u>event</u> in modern Chinese history.
8	Waste is <u>naturally</u> extracted via the kidney tubules. This may not be possible, however, if the kidneys have been damaged.	Waste is <u>normally</u> extracted via the kidney tubules. This may not be possible, however, if the kidneys have been damaged.
9	It is hoped that within the next 10 years educating boys in preference to girls will no longer be <u>normative</u>.	It is hoped that within the next 10 years educating boys in preference to girls will no longer be the <u>norm</u>.
10	Avian flu has <u>spread vastly</u>.	Avian flu has <u>become widespread</u>.

15 Advantage or disadvantage, plenty or too much, enough or not enough, presence or absence

15.1 Words in action

Advantage

▸ The idea of competitive <u>advantage</u> as a key management tool has been criticised.

▸ There are three main <u>benefits</u> to using anti-spyware software.

▸ The voting capacity of the US 'blue states' is <u>a boon</u> to democratic candidates.

▸ There is some <u>merit</u> in using a cognitive behavioural approach.

Disadvantage

▸ The advantages of using English as a global language do not outweigh the <u>disadvantages</u>.

▸ The public are often not told about the <u>drawbacks</u> of anti-spyware software.

▸ Using gross domestic product as an economic measure has severe <u>limitations</u>.

▸ There are significant <u>difficulties with / problems with</u> using blanket pesticides.

▸ The report highlighted major <u>shortcomings</u> in the laboratory's testing procedures.

Too much

▸ The investigation found that the police had used <u>excessive</u> force during the riot.

▸ The <u>excess of / surplus of / surfeit of / glut of / oversupply of</u> sugar is driving down market prices.

▸ Toran-Allerand (2004) reviews the <u>plethora of</u> oestrogen receptors in the brain.

▸ People with an <u>over</u>developed sense of competitiveness have a higher incidence of chest pain.

Plenty of

▸ There <u>is an abundance of</u> literature on this issue.

▸ Beeche's report gives / provides <u>ample</u> evidence of coastal water flow input.

Enough or good enough

▸ The right to <u>adequate</u> housing is enshrined in the International Covenant on ESC Rights.

▸ We now have <u>sufficient / enough</u> data to determine the exact source of the radiation.

Not enough or not good enough

▸ Research points to child-raising as a factor in the <u>dearth of / lack of / paucity of // small number of</u> women in science.

▸ Young et al. (2008) argue that there is a <u>scarcity / lack</u> of available outlets for scientific research.

▸ This report reviews the literature on skills <u>shortages</u>.

▸ The team <u>do not have sufficient / have insufficient</u> funding to continue their research.

▸ <u>Depletion of</u> fossil fuel resources is now a major global concern.

▸ Sever magnesium <u>deficiency</u> can lead to diabetes and heart failure.

▸ We <u>underestimated</u> the degree of nervousness the participants would feel.

▸ Kleinhans argues that housing diversification is not enough to prevent social <u>deprivation</u>.

▸ The policy gives students from <u>disadvantaged / deprived</u> backgrounds greater access to funding.

▸ <u>Inadequate</u> legal representation is thought to be a factor in US death penalty cases.

Presence or absence

▸ Witmer and Singer (1999) show that in a virtual environment, the <u>presence of</u> a feeling of reality reduces motion sickness.

▸ Vitamin supplements are important in the <u>absence of</u> fresh vegetables in the diet.

15.2   Information to help you use these words correctly

adequate adj	= Good enough or large enough. E.g. The school has adequate facilities.
	✎ (An) Adequate **care** // **housing** // **schooling** // **diet**.
advantage n **advantageous** adj	= n – A benefit.
	Gr n – An/The **advantage of** X **is** that … The UK has **an advantage over** the US in terms of … **There is an advantage in / to** look**ing** after your health …
	✎ The advantages **outweigh** // **negate** the disadvantages.
	✱ The word *pro* is too informal for academic writing.
ample adj	= Enough or more than enough of something.
	✎ Ample **evidence of** // **proof of** // **research on** // **justification for** // **scope for** // **supply of** // **quantity of** // **space for** // **capacity**.

boon n	= (1) A benefit. Similar to *advantage*. (2) A favour or request.
dearth n	= A severe or total lack of something.
deficiency n **deficient** adj	= n – (1) A lack of something in the body. E.g. A vitamin deficiency. (2) A fault or inadequate standard. E.g. The report highlighted the government's deficiencies. *Gr* adj – The agency was found to have been **deficient in** its handling of the case.
deplete v **depletion** n	= v – To reduce of to use up (almost) completely. *Gr* n – The depletion **of** resources.
deprived adj **deprivation** n	= adj – Lacking the necessities for a comfortable standard of living. Similar to *disadvantaged*. 𝒫 A deprived **childhood** // **neighbourhood** // **area**. **Economically** // **culturally** // **socially** deprived. ≠ *Deprived / deprivation* and *depraved / depravation* *Depraved / depravation* have the very different meaning of being immoral / immorality.
disadvantage n / v **disadvantaged** adj	= n – Something that is not beneficial. v – To put someone into an unbeneficial situation. adj – Socially and economically poor. Similar to *deprived*. 𝒫 n – A **distinct / definite** // **major / significant** // **slight** // **economic** // **political** disadvantage. To **address** // **alleviate** // **overcome** // **outweigh** a disadvantage. To **feel / be at** a disadvantage. The disadvantages **outweigh** // **negate** the advantages. 𝒫 adj – A disadvantaged **background** // **childhood** // **neighbourhood** // **area**. **Economically** // **culturally** // **socially** disadvantaged. ✱ The opposite of *disadvantaged* is *privileged*, not *advantaged*. The word *con* is too informal for academic writing.

glut n	= Too much of something, usually used in the context of food and other market commodities. Similar to *excess, surplus, surfeit*.
inadequate adj	= Not good enough or large enough. E.g. The standard of work is inadequate.
	ℰ Inadequate **care** // **housing** // **schooling**. An inadequate **job** // **diet**.
insufficient adj	= Not enough in number or amount.
	ℰ Insufficient **research** // **data** // **evidence** // **proof** // **information** // **knowledge** // **understanding** // **energy** // **force** // **strength**.
	≠ *Insufficient* and *inadequate* These words can sometimes be interchanged but, as shown here, *insufficient* means that there is/are not enough of something, while *inadequate* usually means that something is not good enough.
merit n / v	= n – The value, worth, advantage, positive features or excellence of something. v – To be worth doing or to deserve.
	Gr n – **The merit of** the theory is that … There is **merit in** repeating the test. This essay will discuss **the merits of** the Internet. Note that *merit* can be both singular (meaning 'value') and plural (meaning 'advantages' or 'positive features') as shown above.
	ℰ n – To **judge / assess** // **question / investigate** // **consider** // **compare** // **appreciate** the merits of Y. The research **deserves** merit. There is **little** // **considerable / great** merit in this policy. v – It merits **further investigation** // **attention** // **consideration** // **discussion** // **examination**.
over (prefix)	= The prefix *over* usually means something is done too much or that there is too much of something.
	ℰ v – To **overemphasise** // **oversimplify** // **overestimate** // **overproduce**. adj – X is **overpopulated** // **overpaid** // **overpriced** // **overworked**. n – An **overgeneralisation** // **oversimplification**.

paucity n	= A small amount or number of something or not enough of something in a specific context. E.g. Many Yugoslav names have a *paucity* of vowels.
plethora n	= An oversupply. Similar to *excess* and *surfeit*. *Plethora* is also sometimes used to mean 'a lot of' rather than 'too much'.
	Gr Plethora is a singular noun. E.g. There **is** a plethora of academic articles on the subject.
scarcity n **scarce** adj	= n – A lack of <u>universal</u> supply – not enough. E.g. The scarcity of diamonds is a myth created by the sellers to increase prices.
shortcoming n	= A failure, deficiency or fault.
	≠ *Shortcoming* and *disadvantage* These two words have different meanings and so are not interchangeable. (See above for *disadvantage*.)
sufficient adj	= Enough in number or amount.
	✍ Sufficient **research** // **data** // **evidence** // **proof** // **information** // **knowledge** // **understanding**.
	≠ *Sufficient* and *adequate* These words can sometimes be interchanged but, as shown here, *sufficient* means there is/are enough of something, while *adequate* usually means that something is good enough.
surfeit n	= Too much of something, usually used in the context of food and other market commodities. Similar to *excess*, *surplus* and *glut*.
	Gr There is a **surfeit of** X.
under (prefix)	= The prefix *under* usually means that there is not enough in amount or degree of something.
	✍ v – To **underestimate** // **underperform** // **undervalue** // **underutilise** // **understate** // **underspend**. adj – **Underdeveloped** // **underestimated** // **underfunded**.

15.3 Nearly but not quite right

The sentences on the left contain the types of mistakes people make when using words from this section. The correct versions are given on the right.

	Incorrect	Correct
1	There is still debate about whether the <u>pros</u> of the human population having different blood groups outweigh the <u>cons</u>.	There is still debate about whether the <u>benefits / advantages (merits)</u> of the human population having different blood groups outweigh the <u>disadvantages</u>.
2	Employers are often unwilling to state an employee's <u>disadvantages</u> in a reference.	Employers are often unwilling to state an employee's <u>shortcomings</u> in a reference.
3	The benefits <u>in</u> increasing the product price are outlined below.	The benefits <u>of</u> increasing the product price are outlined below.
4	The <u>advantages</u> for species <u>to have</u> more than one blood group is that it provides opposing selective forces.	The <u>advantage</u> for species <u>of having</u> more than one blood group is that it provides opposing selective forces.
5	The drug was not developed further owing to its <u>abundant</u> side-effects.	The drug was not developed further owing to its <u>many / numerous</u> side-effects.
6	<u>Exceeding</u> Internet use can interfere with normal life.	<u>Excessive</u> Internet use can interfere with normal life.
7	The standard of the auditor's work was <u>insufficient</u>.	The standard of the auditor's work was <u>inadequate</u>.
8	There are many advantages for students <u>to study</u> philosophy.	There are many advantages for students <u>of studying</u> philosophy.
9	Owing to the <u>rarity</u> of engineers with shale blasting skills, the company has decided not to continue operations.	Owing to the <u>lack / scarcity / dearth of</u> engineers with shale blasting skills, the company has decided not to continue operations.
10	Research has shown that students who come from more <u>advantage</u> backgrounds are more likely to pass.	Research has shown that students who come from more <u>privileged / advantageous</u> backgrounds are more likely to pass.

16   Importance, relevance, influence and impact

16.1   Words in action (For *ability* and *capacity*, see section 28.)

Importance and relevance

▸ Play is <u>a crucial / critical / vital / an essential // an indispensable</u> part of childhood.

▸ Reaching an agreement on the treaty amendments is <u>paramount</u>.

▸ The Norman Conquest was a <u>pivotal</u> event in the history of England.

▸ Fishbach (2003) suggests that long-term goals usually <u>override</u> immediate temptations.

▸ *R. v. Sparrow* was a <u>landmark</u> decision on the issue of Canadian aboriginal rights.

▸ In 2008 the Kyoto Protocol was an <u>historic</u> moment in the climate change debate.

▸ The report describes the <u>pressing / urgent</u> need for more foster carers in the UK.

▸ Hand-washing <u>warrants attention</u> because it is a main cause of bacterial transmission.

▸ I will discuss whether safety should always <u>take precedence / have priority</u> over profit.

Of little or no importance or relevance

▸ The police decided that the document was <u>insignificant</u>.

▸ The drug was found to have <u>(only) a marginal / a minor effect on</u> clinical malaria.

▸ The study argues that fathers have (only) a <u>peripheral</u> role in family life.

▸ Despite the media hype, identity cards are in fact <u>tangential</u> to the issue of national security.

▸ Table 1 shows the number of <u>incidental</u> injuries to marine mammals during commercial fishing operations.

Dominance

▸ In the US, large-scale monoculture farming has become the <u>dominant</u> agricultural paradigm.

▸ The chief executive <u>dominated</u> the meeting.

▸ <u>The prevailing</u> opinion among the respondents was that they did not receive sufficient compensation.

▸ The pursuit of wealth sometimes <u>takes precedence / predominates</u> over that of happiness.

▸ <u>The pre-eminent</u> figure of the Bloomsbury Group was Virginia Woolf.

▸ Horace Bristol was <u>an eminent / a prominent</u> figure in American photojournalism.

Influence, impact and pressure (See also section 20 for vocabulary relating to cause and effect.)

▸ Marxist Communism is still an <u>influential</u> ideology despite the breakup of the Soviet Union.

- Morris (1992) states that her work on euthanasia is <u>informed</u> by a feminist perspective.
- In case law, a judgment <u>sets a precedent</u> for future decisions.
- Gurtman (1990) showed that unconscious ageism has an <u>impact on / effect on</u> people's behaviour.
- Research suggests that the new EU regulations will be a <u>catalyst</u> for change in fund management.
- The evidence presented shows that international trade <u>accentuates</u> rather than ameliorates the effects of poverty.
- The dove became a <u>potent</u> symbol in the American post-war peace movement.
- The analysis above shows how toy adverts <u>reinforce</u> gender stereotypes.
- The main goal of the strike action is to <u>put / exert</u> <u>pressure</u> on the government.

Positive impact

- Several recent studies show the <u>positive</u> <u>effect / impact</u> of daily exercise on mental health.
- Genome sequencing would not be possible without recent <u>advances / breakthroughs</u> in computing.
- The launch of the project was seen as a significant <u>achievement</u>.
- The teaching practices within the school are <u>exemplary</u>.
- Rowledge (2011) suggests that having a sustainability policy can promote <u>virtuous circles / virtuous cycles</u> in an organisation.

Negative impact

- Peak oil is likely to have an <u>adverse / negative</u> <u>impact on / effect on</u> the global economy.
- Peak oil is likely to be <u>detrimental to / damaging to</u> the global economy.
- I argue that negative media coverage of individual teenagers has a <u>pernicious / insidious</u> effect on adolescents generally.
- Hitchings shows that urban habitats are <u>inimical</u> to common toad populations.
- The main objection is that the superstore will be <u>prejudicial</u> to smaller, local shops.
- The recent E. Coli outbreak in Europe has <u>undermined</u> public confidence in organic vegetables.
- In his novels Dickens explicitly identifies the <u>vicious circle / vicious cycle</u> of poverty and lack of education.
- The performance targets had the effect of <u>diverting</u> attention <u>away from</u> new safety regulations.
- The many <u>digressions</u> in the essay <u>detract from</u> the main argument.

16.2 Information to help you use these words correctly

accentuate v	= To make more noticeable. Similar to *emphasise* and *highlight*. *Accentuate* is sometimes used less precisely to mean 'increase'.
	≠ X accentuates the **positive aspects** // **negative aspects** // **effect(s)** // **problem** // **role** // **severity** // **differences** // **similarities**.
advance n / v	= n – A positive development or invention. v – To develop or progress.
	ℰ n – A/An **considerable / major / significant / important** advance in **science** // **design** // **medicine** // **technology** // **(our) understanding** // **(our) knowledge**. v – To advance **an agenda** // **a career** // **(our) knowledge** / **(our) understanding**.
	≠ *Advance* and *advance**ment*** *Advancement* usually means professional promotion or other recognised form of career development.
adverse adj	= Bad, unpleasant and/or harmful.
	ℰ An adverse **effect** // **side-effect** // **reaction** // **impact** // **situation** // **outcome** / **consequence**. Adverse **publicity** // **conditions**.
	≠ *Ad**verse*** and *averse* To be *averse* to something means to not like/want something, or to be opposed to something. E.g. Most investors are fundamentally risk-averse.
catalyst n	= Something or someone that causes change, often suddenly.
	Gr **To act as** a catalyst **for** change. **To be** a catalyst **for** improved management.

critical adj	= (1) Essential. (2) Contains an analysis of both the positive and negative aspects, followed by an evaluation. This is the most common use of *critical* in academic writing. E.g. Critical thinking, to critically evaluate. (3) At an extremely important point and/or point of crisis. See also section 4, page 23.
detrimental adj **detriment** n	= adj – Harmful, damaging. *Gr* adj – Pollutants **are** detrimental **to** health. n – Cutting funding will be **to the detriment of** patients. *℘* To have a detrimental **effect on** / **impact on** health.
digress v **digression** n	= v – To move away from the main topic / issue.
divert v **diversion** n	= (1) To cause to change direction or purpose. (2) To take attention away from something else. Similar to *distract*. (See section 25, pages 167 and 168.)
dominant adj **dominance** n **dominate** v	= adj – The most powerful. E.g. Should a leader be the dominant person in a group? = n – Greater power. E.g. Should a leader have dominance over the group? = v – To exert power. E.g. Should a leader always try to dominate the group?
eminent adj	= (Of people) admired and respected in their field.
exemplary adj	= Acting as an excellent example or model.

historic adj	= Interesting and important because of its history. E.g. Rome is an historic city. Today's ruling is an historic moment in the campaign.
	≠ *Historic* and *historical* These two words have different meanings. *Historical* merely means 'relating to history' not that the place/event/person is necessarily important. E.g. I am doing a small amount of historical research. There is no evidence that the historical Dick Wittington had a cat.
	* *An historic/al* and *a historic/al* are both acceptable.
impact n / v	= n – The effect or action on something else.
	Gr n – *Impact* is always singular and used with *on* + noun. E.g. **The impact/s of** poverty can be serious. ✗ Poverty can have serious **impacts on** health. ✗ Poverty can have **a serious impact on** health. ✓
	✎ To **soften** / **cushion** / **lessen** // **minimise** // **absorb** the impact of X.
	≠ *Effect* and *impact* These words have similar meanings but *impact* is often used for changes that are more sudden or dramatic.
incidental adj	= Occurring by chance as part of something else and/or of minor importance or with minor effect.
inform v	= (1) To give information. (2) To influence the attitude, opinion or style of someone/something. This is a common use of *inform* in academic writing. E.g. Their designs are informed by their experience of living and working in China.
inimical adj	= Harmful and/or obstructive. Similar to *detrimental*.
insidious adj	= Having a gradual, harmful effect. Similar to *pernicious*.

landmark adj / n	= adj – Extremely significant. Usually used to describe an event, action, development or stage in a process. n – (1) A significant action or event which acts as a turning point. E.g. Ibn al-Nafis' explanation of blood circulation in 1242 was a landmark in biological science. (2) An easily recognisable feature of the landscape.
	✐ adj – X is / represents a landmark **ruling** // **decision** // **event** // **study** // **discovery** // **novel** // **essay**.
marginal adj	= Of minor importance or very small. For *marginalise* see section 13, page 81.
overriding adj **override** v	= adj – The most important. v – (1)To use authority to cancel or reject something. (2)To be more important than anything else.
	✐ adj – The overriding **aim** / **goal** / **objective** // **factor** // **principle** // **concern** // **consideration** // **priority** is X. X is of overriding **importance** // **significance**.
paramount adj	= More important than anything else.
	Gr X **is** paramount. **It is** paramount **that** …
peripheral adj **periphery** n	= adj – On the outer edges, marginal or of minor importance.
	✐ X is **of** peripheral **importance to** Y. X **plays** a peripheral **role in** Y.
pernicious adj	= Evil, wicked and/or having a harmful effect, often gradually. Similar to *insidious*.
pivotal adj	= Extremely significant and/or leading to great change.
	✐ X **plays a** pivotal **role in** Y. Abraham Lincoln **is a** pivotal **figure** in American history.
precedence n	= Being more important than something else. E.g. Should happiness take precedence over wealth?
	✐ X **takes precedence over** Y.

precedent n	= Something that acts as an example, standard or decisive ruling for something else. E.g. The sacking of the minister sets a worrying precedent.
	⏀ To **set a** precedent. A **legal** // **historical** // **historic** // **constitutional** precedent. The ruling **is / provides / serves as / constitutes** a precedent for the future.
	≠ *Prece*dent and *presi*dent These similar sounding words have very different meanings.
	✱ The adjective *unprecedented* means 'never happened before'. (See section 7, page 47.)
predominant adj **predominance** n **predominate** v **predominantly** adv	= adj – (1) The main, largest or most common. E.g. The predominant colour in the tapestry was red. (2) The most common and therefore most powerful. E.g. The predominant opinion was that the treaty should be signed.
pre-eminent adj	= The best, most important or most influential within a specific context. Usually used for people.
prejudicial adj	= (1) Harmful, detrimental. (2) Being or having prejudice/d or bias/ed. (3) Leading to premature judgement (usually used in the context of law).
prevailing adj **prevail** n	= adj – (1) The most influential or dominant behaviour or attitude. (2) Existing at a particular place and time (often the present).
	⏀ The/A prevailing **attitude** // **custom** // **trend** // **belief** // **ideology** // **mood** // **opinion** // **assumption**. The prevailing **circumstances** // **conditions** // **climate** // **situation** // **rate** // **value**.
tangential adj **tangent** n	= adj – (1) Of little or no relevance or importance. (2) In geometry, along a tangent.

undermine v	=	To cause something to become less successful, powerful, secure or confident. (See also section 12, page 78 and section 25, page 171.)
	✐	To undermine **authority** // **confidence**.
warrant v	=	To necessitate, justify or deserve.

16.3 Nearly but not quite right

The sentences on the left contain the types of mistakes people make when using words from this section. The correct versions are given on the right.

	Incorrect	Correct
1	Britain's first televised campaign debate in 2010 was an <u>historical</u> event.	Britain's first televised campaign debate in 2010 was an <u>historic</u> event.
2	The report emphasised that a desire for results should not <u>preside</u> over accuracy.	The report emphasised that a desire for results should not <u>take precedence over</u> accuracy.
3	In law, <u>pre-eminent</u> figures should be treated in the same way as anyone else.	In law, <u>prominent</u> figures should be treated in the same way as anyone else.
4	Clinical trials <u>are a pivotal role for</u> the development of treatment drugs.	Clinical trials <u>play a pivotal role</u> in the development of treatment drugs.
5	The <u>impacts of</u> computer technology are only just starting to be fully realised.	The <u>effects</u> of computer technology are only just starting to be fully realised.
6	There is a dearth of literature on the <u>averse impacts of</u> drugs on job performance.	There is a dearth of literature on the <u>adverse impact of</u> drugs on job performance.
7	The army <u>was predominant over</u> the region for fifteen years.	The army <u>dominated</u> the region for fifteen years.
8	Newspapers often fail to explain <u>advances of</u> science clearly.	Newspapers often fail to explain <u>advances in</u> science clearly.
9	The new vaccine <u>is very potent</u> for preventing HIV.	The new vaccine <u>has great potential</u> for preventing HIV.
10	The ruling sets a <u>president</u> for future libel actions.	The ruling sets a <u>precedent</u> for future libel actions.

Communication, expression, understanding, way of thinking and point of view

● ● ● ● ● ●

17 Communication, expression, signification and portrayal

17.1 Words in action

Transmitting information

▸ Technology has allowed radical new ways of <u>communicating</u>.

▸ Beacco et al. (2002) argue that knowledge is not <u>transmitted</u> only in one direction from scientists to the public.

▸ This essay will evaluate different ways in which scientific innovations are <u>disseminated</u>.

▸ A molecular formula <u>conveys</u> information about the chemical's atomic structure.

▸ The NATO-Russia Council is a <u>mechanism for</u> consultation and cooperation.

▸ Psychologists claim that blogging is now the most popular <u>vehicle</u> for self-expression.

▸ The book provides a descriptive <u>account of</u> the theory of Marxism.

Different ways of communicating and expressing emotion

▸ A translation that is too <u>literal</u> will often read as plodding and unnatural.

▸ The authors criticise the government <u>implicitly</u> in their report.

▸ I will argue that the government gave its <u>tacit</u> approval to the project.

▸ In *Two Gentlemen of Verona*, Shakespeare <u>alludes to</u> the Greek myth of Hero and Leander.

▸ Conflict <u>euphemisms</u> such as 'collateral damage' serve to distance us from the consequences of war.

▸ The use of a melting pot as a <u>metaphor</u> for immigrant assimilation in US cities is no longer valid.

▸ According to the World Health Organisation, developing regions need more <u>explicit</u> health policies.

▸ Violent acts are one type of <u>overt</u> aggression in the workplace described by Baron and Neuman (1996).

▸ In the poem 'Do not go gentle into that good night', Thomas <u>expresses</u> his emotions at watching his father die.

- *The Vanishing Princess* stories (Diski, 1995) <u>convey</u> brilliantly a sense of wasted life and self-entrapment.
- Anger can <u>manifest itself</u> in various ways, including violent and destructive behaviour.

Signification

- The coming down of the Berlin wall in 1989 <u>signified / represented</u> the end of the Cold War.
- The announcement by the government <u>denotes / signifies</u> a change in policy.
- For Dickens' character Pip in *Great Expectations*, the prison ship <u>embodies</u> menace and evil.

Depiction and portrayal

- I suggest that the <u>portrayal of / representation of</u> some teenagers as 'hoodies' is harmful to society as a whole.
- I will argue that the report <u>projects</u> an overly negative <u>image of</u> drug use.
- A carving <u>depicting / showing / representing</u> a mammoth has recently been found on a bone fragment in Florida.

17.2   Information to help you use these words correctly

allude v allusion n	=	v – To suggest indirectly or to mention only briefly. n – A phrase that makes an indirect reference to something else.
	≠	*Allude* and *elude* *To elude* is (1) to escape capture / danger or (2) to not be remembered or understood. E.g. 'The name of the play escapes / eludes me.'
	≠	*Allusion* and *illusion* An i**l**lusion is a false idea, belief or visual phenomenon.
convey v	=	(1) To communicate and/or express an idea or feeling. (2) To transport or carry.
	Gr	Convey + indirect object or noun (not *that*). E.g. Larkin conveys that ... ✗ Larkin conveys **the idea** that ... ✓
	⌀	To convey (a/an) **emotion // feelings // idea // information // a sense of** X.
denote v	=	To indicate or to show. *Denote* is often used in the context of formulations. E.g. In the equation, S and Q denote mutation and polymorphism respectively.

depict v **depiction** n	= v – (1) To describe something using pictures or words. E.g. The painting depicts a rural scene in the 17th century. (2) To characterise or show in a particular way. Similar to *portray*. E.g. In the novel he is depicted as an evil scientist.
disseminate v **dissemination** n	= v – To spread over a wide area. ≠ To disseminate **information** // **news** // **stories** // **research** // **ideas** // **knowledge** // **propaganda**. To disseminate **by / via email** // **the Internet** // **newspaper**.
embody v **embodiment** n	= v – (1) To give physical / tangible form to something. (2) To be a good (or best) example of an idea, principle, belief or quality. (3) To contain or include.
euphemism n **euphemistic** adj **euphemistically** adv	= n – An indirect or mild expression used as a substitution for something thought to be too blunt or offensive. E.g. He passed away last week. = He died last week. I am in between jobs. = I am unemployed.
explicit adj **explicitly** adv	= adj – (1) Clear and obvious. (2) Depicting sexual activity. ✐ (An) explicit **instruction** // **threat** // **example** // **warning**.
express v / adj	= v – To convey a feeling, thought or idea. adj – Very clear. E.g. She gave her express permission. The express purpose of the meeting was to finalise the deal.
implicit adj **implicitly** adv	= adj (1) Expressed indirectly. Similar to *tacit*. (2) An essential and logical part of something. E.g. Death is an implicit part of life. (3) Total and unquestioning. E.g. An implicit faith in God. ✐ (An) implicit **acknowledgement** // **agreement** // **assumption** // **recognition** // **understanding**. Implicit **criticism** // **critique** // **challenge** // **condemnation**.

literal adj **literally** adv	=	adj – The surface or 'word for word' meaning of something.
	𝒪	**In a / the literal sense**. The **literal meaning of** X is Y.
	≠	*Literally* and *literary*. *Literally* is the adverb of *literal*. E.g. A parable should not be read literally but as an illustration of a principle. *Literary* is an adjective meaning 'related to literature and writing'. E.g. Jane Austen is a famous literary figure.
	*	The adjective *literate* can mean either 'able to read and write' or 'well-educated'.
manifest v / adj	=	v – To show in a particular way or form. E.g. The AHS virus manifests itself in four different forms. adj – Clear and obvious. E.g. The report highlights the research study's manifest flaws.
	Gr	v – X **manifests itself as** Y. X **manifests itself in (the form of)** Y.
mechanism	=	The thing or process by which something else happens. In academic study, *mechanism* is commonly used for non-mechanical contexts. E.g. The report evaluates democratic mechanisms for taxation.
	Gr	X is a mechanism **for consultation**. X is a mechanism **by which** members consult and cooperate.
metaphor n	=	Using the image of one thing to represent another. E.g. He is a lion stalking its prey in the urban jungle.
	≠	*Metaphor*, *simile* and *analogy* A simile also uses images to compare things, but uses *like or as* (and so is often less powerful than a metaphor). E.g. He is **like** a lion stalking its prey. My love is **as** deep **as** the ocean. An analogy is a comparison (using either simile or metaphor) that is explained as part of an argument. (See also the introduction to section 21 and page 137.)

overt adj	= Open and obvious rather than hidden. Similar to *explicit*. ℮ Overt **behaviour** // **support** // **racism** // **hostility** // **aggression**. ≠ *Overt* and *covert* C*overt* means 'hidden' or 'secret' and so has the opposite meaning to *overt*. However, *covert* is usually used in a military context. For academic writing use *indirect*, *implicit* or *tacit* rather than *covert*.
portray v **portrayal** n	= v – (1) To describe or show in a book or film. E.g. The book graphically portrays the horror of the First World War. (2) To describe in a particular way or with particular characteristics. E.g. The film portrays him **as** evil. *Gr* Portray + object or noun (not *that*). E.g. He portrayed that … ✗ The film portrays **him** as evil. ✓ Often used with **as** and often in the passive. E.g. In the film he **is portrayed as** an evil scientist. ℮ v – X **accurately** // **faithfully** // **powerfully** // **vividly** // **starkly** // **sympathetically** // **sensitively** // **falsely** // **misleadingly** portrays Y. n – X gives a(n) **accurate** // **faithful** // **powerful** … portrayal of Y.
project v / n	= v – (1) To give a particular impression or image. E.g. The company projects a wholesome image. (2) To depict or convey a particular message or meaning. (3) To forecast using current information. (See section 26, page 180.) ✻ The verb is pronounced to pro<u>ject</u> and the noun is pronounced a <u>pro</u>ject.
represent v	= (1) To symbolise or indicate something. Similar to *signify*. (2) To describe or show in a book, film or work of art using pictures or words. Similar to *depict* and *portray*. (3) To amount to / be the equivalent of.
signify v	= To symbolise or indicate something. Similar to *denote* and meaing (1) above of *represent*.

tacit adj	= Expressed in an indirect or hidden way. Similar to *implicit*.
	✐ To give tacit **agreement** // **approval** // **acknowledgement** // **consent** // **support**. To **have** // **gain** tacit **knowledge of** X.
transmit v	= To pass on information, attitude or beliefs. Similar to *communicate* but with more emphasis on passing on something to another specific person, group or place.
	✐ To transmit **knowledge** // **data** // **information** // **values** // **ideas** // **beliefs** // **attitudes**.
vehicle n	= Something that allows something else to be expressed or fulfilled.

17.3 Nearly but not quite right

The sentences on the left contain the types of mistakes people make when using words from this section. The correct versions are given on the right.

	Incorrect	Correct
1	English is an <u>implicit</u> subject when studying for a degree.	English is an <u>important</u> subject when studying for a degree. or (with a different meaning) <u>It is implied / It is assumed</u> that you use English when studying for a degree.
2	I need to improve the way I <u>express my ideas across</u>.	I need to improve the way I <u>convey / transmit / communicate</u> my ideas.
3	Companies need to <u>convey their message across to</u> consumers.	Companies need to <u>convey / transmit / communicate their message to</u> consumers.
4	The ideas <u>portrayed</u> in the report are not new.	The ideas <u>conveyed / transmitted / communicated</u> in the report are not new.
5	The poem contains <u>metaphors</u> relating to colour, for example 'as black as midnight'.	The poem contains <u>similes</u> relating to colour, for example 'as black as midnight'

	Incorrect	Correct
6	The discrimination people face <u>is through</u> various forms.	The discrimination people face is <u>manifested / expressed / shown</u> in various forms.
7	Fundamentalist groups place great emphasis on the <u>literary</u> meaning of their founding texts.	Fundamentalist groups place great emphasis on the <u>literal</u> meaning of their founding texts.
8	One school of thought states that teaching should always be <u>informed with</u> research.	One school of thought states that teaching should always be <u>informed by</u> research.
9	The minister attended the rally on the <u>expressed</u> understanding that she would leave at the first sign of violence.	The minister attended the rally on the <u>express</u> understanding that she would leave at the first sign of violence.
10	It can be clearly <u>manifested</u> that the results are similar to those of our previous study.	It can clearly be <u>seen</u> that the results are similar to those of our previous study. As <u>is</u> clearly <u>shown</u>, the results are similar to those of our previous study.

18   Knowledge, understanding, perception, way of thinking and belief

18.1   Words in action

Knowledge, ignorance and mental process

- We do not yet have adequate <u>knowledge about</u> how these types of infection are spread.
- A growing number of children <u>are ignorant of / are unaware of / have no awareness of // have little awareness of</u> how food is grown.
- Dickens <u>conceived</u> the plot for *A Tale of Two Cities* while acting in a play.
- Memory is one of the key <u>cognitive processes</u> involved in language learning.

Understanding and misunderstanding

- Fractals (infinitely repeating geometric shapes) can be <u>understood on</u> several <u>different levels</u>.
- This survey <u>provides fresh insights into / gives us a better understanding of</u> why people smoke.
- Viewing Skinner's 'negative reinforcement' as punishment is a common <u>misconception / misunderstanding</u>.
- Johnson (1988) argues that Reagan's policy of supporting 'freedom fighters' was <u>misguided</u>.

Interpretation, perception and connotation

- Sloboda and Lehmann (2001) investigate how listeners <u>interpret</u> the same piece of music differently.
- Legislation is often <u>open to interpretation</u> and so the principle of statutory construction is important.
- Avoiding eye contact is <u>perceived as / seen as</u> a sign of shyness in Western cultures.
- Our <u>perception</u> of reality, according to Clark, is shaped via a cycle of expectation, experience and mental modification.
- Working-class speech patterns have more favourable <u>connotations / associations</u> for men than for women.

Way of thinking, ideology and belief

- Many psychologists today do not adhere closely to any one <u>school of thought</u>.
- We need to go back and examine the problem from a <u>theoretical</u> perspective.
- The renewal of the weapons contracts is seen by some as a <u>pragmatic</u> approach to global economics.
- The new Environmental <u>Paradigm</u> Scale is used to measure attitudes to the environment.
- Caspi and Roberts argue that mental <u>constructs</u> can be changed in adulthood and even old age.
- The belief that Jesus is the son of God forms the basis of Christian <u>dogma</u>.

- Marxist Communism is still an influential <u>ideology</u>, despite the breakup of the Soviet Union.
- The Peter <u>Principle</u> states that successful employees are eventually promoted to a level beyond their capability.
- The main <u>tenet</u> of Christian Science is that God's creation is entirely good, and that evil is an illusion.
- The Health <u>Belief</u> Model attempts to predict and explain people's health behaviours.

18.2   Information to help you use these words correctly

conceive v	= (1) To form or create an idea or plan in the mind. (2) To become pregnant.
	Gr To conceive the idea **of** doing X. To conceive the idea **for** X.
	ℰ To conceive an **idea** // **concept** / **notion** // **project** // **plan**. X is **well** // **poorly** conceived.
connotation n	= An emotion or idea associated with a word or phrase in addition to its literal meaning. Similar to *association*.
	ℰ A **positive** // **negative** // **strong** // **obvious** // **subtle** connotation.
construct n / v	= n – A complex idea made by combining different pieces of knowledge or different concepts. v – To build, develop or create. E.g. He constructs his argument carefully and logically.
	ℰ n – A **theoretical** // **abstract** // **mental** construct.
dogma n **dogmatic** adj	= n – A system of principles or beliefs that are viewed as undeniably true, held by a religious group. *Dogma* is also sometimes used more loosely to refer to very strong political views. adj – (1) Relating to dogma. (2) The characteristic of being stubborn and opinionated, refusing to consider any other point of view, even in the face of seemingly contradictory evidence.

ideology n **ideological** adj **ideologically** adv	= n – A set of ideas held by a social or political group used to promote and/or protect their interests. ⌀ A **political** // **liberal** // **extremist** // **free-market** // **secular** // **racist** // **totalitarian** ideology. The **dominant** / **ruling** / **prevailing** ideology. To **adopt** // **embrace** // **share** // **challenge** // **oppose** an ideology.
insight n **insightful** adj	= n – A new understanding or piece of new knowledge arising as a result of bringing different ideas together. (See also section 24, page 158.) ⌀ **Fresh** // **further** // **new** // **rare** // **unique** // **profound** // **clear** // **useful** // **important** // **valuable** insight(s). To **give** // **acquire** // **obtain** // **present** // **provide** // **offer** // **afford** (an) insight(s) into X.
interpret v **interpretation** n	= v – To explain or understand the meaning of something.
knowledge n	= Awareness: ideas or information that have not been disproved. 𝒢𝓇 There is a difference in meaning between **knowledge of** and **knowledge about**. **Knowledge of** means knowledge that the item, topic or issue exists. E.g. 'I had no knowledge of the report' means that I did not know that the report existed. **Knowledge about** means knowledge of the details or particular aspects within an item, topic or issue. E.g. 'I had no knowledge about the report' means that I knew the report existed but not what it contained.
misconception n **misconceive** v	= n – An incorrect belief or opinion caused by a lack of understanding. ⌀ To **have** / **hold** / **labour under** the misconception that … The misconception **exists** // **persists** that … To **address** / **tackle** / **confront** // **counter** / **challenge** the misconception that … X **reinforces** // **perpetuates** // **gives rise to** / **leads to** the misconception that … A **common** // **popular** // **prevalent** // **widespread** // **damaging** // **fundamental** / **basic** misconception is …

misguided adj **misguide** v	= adj – Misjudged or incorrect. Usually used in the context of actions, beliefs or opinions. v – To mislead.
	✐ A misguided **attempt** // **assumption** // **belief** // **impression** // **perception**.
paradigm n	= (1) An overarching framework, set of ideas or world view that underpins and directs an area of theory and/or research. E.g. Quantum mechanics presents a paradigm shift in the study of sub-atomic physics. (2) A typical and/or excellent example of something.
perceive v **perception** n	= v – (1) To see or become aware of something. (2) To understand or realise something in a particular way.
pragmatic adj **pragmatism** n	= adj – Related to real-world reasoning and results rather than to abstract theory. n – (1) An approach whereby things are judged and valued on the basis of their real-world effects rather than by preconceived beliefs or ideas. (2) A theory of knowledge that looks at how theory and practice affect each other.
	✐ A pragmatic **approach** // **attitude** // **stance** // **perspective** // **view** // **strategy** // **policy**.
	≠ *Pragmatic* and *practical* These words can sometimes be interchanged but they do have different meanings. *Pragmatic* relates to <u>thinking</u> about real-world reasoning and effects, while *practical* relates to how you actually put this thinking into practice. For *practical* and *practicable* see section 28, page 193.
principle n	= A belief, idea, theory, rule or moral code. E.g. Elections should be based on egalitarian principles.
	≠ *Principle* and *principal* *Principal* means the main and/or most important. E.g. The principal aim of the legislation is to reduce crime.
school of **thought** n	= A point of view or ideology held by an authoritative group. E.g. Post-Keynesian and New-Keynesian are different schools of thought within the general Keynesian model.

| tenet n | = A key principle or belief. Usually used in the context of philosophy and religion. |

18.3   Nearly but not quite right

The sentences on the left contain the types of mistakes people make when using words from this section. The correct versions are given on the right.

	Incorrect	Correct
1	The idea of using a computer program to collectively edit a website was <u>perceived</u> by Beck in the 1990s.	The idea of using a computer program to collectively edit a website was <u>conceived</u> by Beck in the 1990s.
2	Rinzai Zen is <u>a way of thinking</u> based in the Japanese rather than the Chinese Zen tradition.	Rinzai Zen is a <u>school of thought</u> based in the Japanese rather than the Chinese Zen tradition.
3	Linguistic identity is the <u>believe</u> that a cultural connection exists between people who share a language.	Linguistic identity is the <u>belief</u> that a cultural connection exists between people who share a language.
4	The report states that the government needs to have a more <u>practical</u> strategy for dealing with inflation.	The report states that the government needs to have a more <u>pragmatic</u> strategy for dealing with inflation.
5	I will firstly summarise the main <u>tenants</u> of Islam.	I will firstly summarise the main <u>tenets</u> of Islam.
6	Wallace believes that the theory of evolution is based on five <u>useful misconceptions</u>.	Wallace believes that the theory of evolution is based on five <u>basic / fundamental misconceptions.</u>
7	The research findings <u>have insights</u> into ways of increasing citizen participation in community projects.	The research findings <u>provide / offer / give us</u> <u>insights</u> into ways of increasing citizen participation in community projects.
8	It is now generally agreed that the action of deploying troops was <u>misconceived</u>.	It is now generally agreed that the action of deploying troops was <u>misguided</u>.
9	Cognitivism is one of the most influential <u>schools of thinking</u> within psychology.	Cognitivism is one of the most influential <u>schools of thought</u> within psychology.
10	There is a public <u>perception of</u> e-books <u>being</u> extremely cheap to produce.	There is a public <u>perception that</u> e-books <u>are</u> extremely cheap to produce.

19 Position, point of view, support and opposition, impartiality and bias

One of the most important aspects of academic study is to be able to understand, describe and analyse the different viewpoints people hold.

Section 19 gives you words and phrases for describing and discussing position and point of view. See also sections 23–26 for analysing and evaluating the views of other authors and for stating your own position.

19.1   Words in action

Position

The article criticises the government's <u>stance / position</u> on potential strike action.

▸ Increasingly, schools are <u>positioning</u> themselves <u>within</u> a free market economy.
▸ The book looks at the medieval Christian crusades <u>from the perspective of</u> the Muslim world.
▸ Personal blogs are written from a purely subjective <u>standpoint</u>.
▸ Increasingly, schools are <u>orientating</u> themselves <u>towards</u> a free market economy.
▸ The study looks at salt sensitivity in the Japanese population <u>from the viewpoint of</u> genetic diversity.

Points of view

▸ <u>The view that</u> all research should be concerned with developing theory <u>is</u> debatable, according to May (2000).
▸ This essay <u>takes the view that</u> earning money from money is unethical.
▸ It is important to analyse the facts before <u>formulating a view</u>.
▸ Many people <u>think / hold the opinion / are of the opinion</u> that using animals for experimentation is inhumane.
▸ Picasso <u>is</u> widely <u>regarded as / viewed as / thought of as / considered to be</u> a major influence in twentieth-century art.

Views that agree, support, argue for or accept

▸ There <u>is</u> cross-party <u>agreement on</u> the issue of identification cards.
▸ After a five-hour meeting the board <u>reached a consensus</u> on the proposals.
▸ I am a <u>proponent of / advocate of / supporter of</u> civil liberties in the UK.
▸ Many alternative health centres <u>endorse</u> homeopathy.
▸ Smith is a leading <u>exponent</u> of permaculture and runs related workshops across the country.
▸ Research literature supports the idea that a successful organisation is one that <u>embraces</u> change.

- Diehm and Armatas (2004) look at how surfing is a high-risk activity that has been <u>accepted by</u> society.
- Most physicists <u>admit / acknowledge / concede / accept</u> that producing a unified theory is a long-term endeavour.
- A poll last year showed that 61 per cent of Americans <u>condoned</u> capital punishment in cases of murder.
- We <u>tolerate</u> a high level of road deaths because we view them as an inevitable consequence of car ownership.

Views that disagree or oppose

- Plans to have a single EU military headquarters have caused <u>disagreement / discord</u> among member states.
- The main <u>objections</u> to the airport proposal are noise, nuisance and damage to wildlife habitat.
- Nativists <u>object to</u> the idea that we are born as 'blank slates' <u>on the grounds that</u> some beliefs are genetically programmed.
- Dawkins <u>is opposed to / rejects</u> the idea of faith schools.
- The Unionists are <u>against / averse to</u> the idea of Ireland being independent from the UK.
- <u>Opponents of</u> stem cell research argue that there is no moral justification for using and destroying embryonic cells.

Impartiality and bias, prejudgement, rationality, objectivity and subjectivity

- I will argue that good journalism should always be <u>impartial / disinterested</u>.
- The Gall-Peters map attempts to correct the Mercator map's visual <u>bias against</u> southern developing countries.
- Our report shows that food labelling <u>is</u> heavily <u>biased towards</u> the producer rather than the consumer.
- Affirmative action may include the policy of giving <u>preferential</u> treatment to candidates from minority groups.
- <u>Discrimination against</u> infant girls still occurs in some parts of China and India.
- The Atheist Society states that it takes a <u>rational</u> <u>view of</u> the God belief.
- I have shown that it is difficult to have an <u>objective</u> perspective on the ethics of medical research.
- Personal blogs are written from a purely <u>subjective</u> standpoint.
- The Commissioner claimed that Britain has <u>an irrational view of</u> Europe.
- I will argue that aid charity advertising can encourage <u>a distorted view of</u> developing countries.

Rigidity, ambivalence, indifference and alternative views

- The article criticises the government's <u>rigid stance / inflexible position / intransigence</u> on strike action.

- Piper (2001) suggests that the more <u>ambivalent</u> one feels about someone, the less we grieve when they die.
- The recent human rights violations indicate that the government is <u>indifferent</u> to international opinion.
- Many economists remain <u>sceptical</u> about the reliability of qualitative research data.
- Taleb's book shows us an <u>alternative view</u> of some traditional mathematical concepts.
- The artist's work is still considered <u>radical</u>, even though he has been painting for over 50 years.

19.2 Information to help you use these words correctly

acceptable adj **accept** v	= adj – Reasonable, adequate. v – (1) To believe. (2) To agree but grudgingly and/or with some reservations. E.g. People often accept public policies they in fact personally oppose. I accept that God might exist but not that he must exist.
	ℰ adj – **Broadly** // **generally** // **mutually** // **socially** // **politically** // **morally** // **ethically** acceptable. X is **considered / deemed to be / seen as** acceptable.
	≠ *Accept and except* These two words have different meanings. *Except* means 'with the exclusion of'. E.g. We compiled the data using all the surveys except for those returned after the deadline. See also section 9, page 58, for *except* to describe anomalies.
advocate v / n	= v – To actively support. n – A (strong) supporter of something.
	Gr n – An **advocate of** / **advocate for** X.
	ℰ v – To **actively** // **openly** // **strongly** advocate X. n – To be **a keen** // **a passionate** advocate of X.
ambivalent adj **ambivalence** n	= adj – Having mixed or contradictory feelings or ideas about something.
	≠ *Ambivalent and indifferent* These words have different meanings. See below for *indifferent*.

averse adj	= Opposed to
	≠ *Averse* and *adverse* *Adverse* means unpleasant and/or harmful. See section 14, page 86.
bias n **biased** adj	= n – The treatment of something in an unequal and partial manner. adj – To be unequal or unfair.
	Gr n – To **have** a bias **towards** X. adj – To be biased **towards** // **against** X.
	C adj – To be **heavily / strongly** // **positively** // **negatively** // **inherently** biased. To be **culturally** // **ideologically** // **politically** // **racially** biased.
concede v **concession** n	= v – To admit or allow something. n – A bargain or compromise. (See also section 12, page 76, and section 26.)
condone v	= To accept or (reluctantly) agree with or approve of behaviour usually viewed as morally wrong.
	C To condone **behaviour** // **the practice of** // **the action of** // **violence** // **abuse** // **torture** // **murder**.
	≠ *Condone* and *tolerate* *To tolerate* means to put up with something you don't like that actually happens to you or around you.
consensus n **consensual** adj	= n – Agreement among the whole group.
discord n	= Lack of agreement / lack of harmony, or disagreement.

discriminate v **discrimination** n **discriminatory** adj	= v – (1) To be able to make a distinction between two or more things. Similar to *differentiate*. E.g. Tutors want to see that students can discriminate between reliable and unreliable material. (2) To show preference for, or to treat unfairly due to prejudgement. E.g. The insurance policy discriminates in favour of older drivers. n – (1) Differentiation. (2) Unfair treatment due to prejudgement.
	✳ As shown in definition (2) above, the verb *discriminate* can be used in a positive as well as a negative sense. *Discrimination* and *discriminatory*, however, have the negative meaning of unfair treatment, e.g. racial discrimination.
disinterested adj **disinterest** n	= adj – (1) Unbiased, not influenced by self-interest. Similar to *impartial* and *unbiased*. (2) Having no interest in the topic / event.
	≠ *Disinterested* and *uninterested* Note that as shown by (2) above, *disinterested* is sometimes used to mean *uninterested*, i.e. that you are not interested. However, only *disinterested* can be used to mean *impartial*.
embrace v	= To accept and welcome something.
	✐ To **willingly** // **actively** // **wholeheartedly** // **fully** embrace. To embrace (a/an) **change** // **challenge** // **concept** / **notion** / **idea** // **opportunity**.
endorse v **endorsement** n	= v – To publicly support and recommend an idea, belief, action or product.
exponent n	= (1) (Of people) an example, practitioner or representative (and so also probably a supporter) of something. (2) A skilled artist or performer, usually a musician.
	≠ *Exponent* and *proponent* See under *proponent* below.
	✳ *Exponent* has other specialised meanings in maths and linguistics. *Exponential* and *exponentially* have a separate meaning, related to rate of change. See section 11, page 70.

impartial adj	= Not influenced by any particular side, or not favouring one side or view. Similar to *neutral*, *unbiased*, *balanced* and *disinterested*. For *partial*, see page 64.
	✐ To **offer** / **give** impartial **advice** / **guidance**.
indifferent adj **indifference** n	= adj – (1) Lacking interest and/or not caring about something. (2) Average / not very good at something. E.g. She is an indifferent tennis player.
	≠ *Indifferent* and *impartial* These words have different meanings. See above for *impartial*.
intransigent adj **intransigence** n	= adj – Inflexible, unwilling to change one's mind or position.
objection n **object** v / n	= n A reason for disagreeing with or disapproving of something.
	Gr To have an **objection to** something.
	✐ A **chief** / **main** / **primary** / **principal** // **fundamental** // **formal** objection.
	✶ The noun is pronounced <u>ob</u>ject and the verb is pronounced ob<u>ject.</u>
objective adj / n	= adj – Based only on facts and not influenced by feelings or beliefs. n – An aim or goal.
perspective n	= (1) A particular mental position or way of thinking from which a view on a specific issue is formed. E.g. I will discuss personal identity from a social behavourist perspective. Similar to *position*, *standpoint* and *viewpoint*. (2) Representation of three-dimensional space on a two-dimensional surface.
preferential adj **preference** n **prefer** v	= adj – Giving advantage to or favouring a person or group over others. n – (1) Advantage given or favour shown to a person or group over others. E.g. Preference is given to applicants who have previous experience. (2) A greater liking. E.g. My preference is for unseen exams rather than continuous assessment.

proponent n	=	Someone who puts forward or is in favour of a plan, idea or theory. Similar to *advocate* and *supporter*.
	≠	*Proponent* and *exponent* The two words are sometimes used interchangeably but there is a difference in meaning. A proponent is in favour of an idea but does not necessarily make their support public or act on it (often because it is an idea or theory, not something they can practically do). An exponent is in favour of something and also does something about it.
radical adj / n	=	adj – (1) Fundamental and/or large. (See section 11, page 71.) (2) Extreme, very different from the norm. (See section 18, page 112. (3) Promoting fundamental political and social change.
	✐	A radical **approach** // **idea** // **policy** // **ideology**. Radical **views**.
regard v / n	=	v – To consider or think of something or someone in a particular way. n – (1) Care or attention given to something or someone. (2) With reference or connection to something or someone. E.g. In regard to ethics. (See section 6, page 36.)
	Gr	n – To **pay** / **give** regard **to** X. To **show** / **have** regard **for** X.
	✐	v – X is **commonly** / **widely** / **generally** / **usually** / **normally** // **traditionally** // **rightly** / **justly** regarded as … n – X has **the utmost** // **a high** // **a low** regard **for** Y. X **pays sufficient** // **insufficient** // **little** / **scant** regard to Y.
sceptical adj **scepticism** n	=	adj – (1) Doubtful. (2) Questioning. In philosophy, scepticism is the approach whereby all knowledge and belief is questioned.
stance n	=	A clear position on something.
	✐	A **hardline** / **tough** // **firm** // **ethical** // **moral** stance on X. To **have** // **adopt** // **hold** // **take** a stance **on** / **against** X.

subjective adj	=	Based on your feelings and beliefs rather than evidence or fact. Opposite of *objective*.
	🖉	The newspaper article is **highly / extremely / largely // somewhat** subjective. A subjective **opinion // viewpoint // response // assessment // judgement**.
view v / n	=	n – An opinion, belief or attitude, often not based on evidence. v – (1) To think of in a particular way. (2) To look at or inspect. This is formal use of *view*. E.g. We viewed the landscape through binoculars.
	🖉	A **personal // broad // narrow // simplistic // orthodox // traditional** view. To **subscribe to / hold** a particular view. X **reflects the view that** …
viewpoint n	=	A particular way of thinking about something. Similar to *standpoint* and *perspective*.
	≠	*Viewpoint, view* and *point of view* These words are often used interchangeably but strictly speaking, a *viewpoint* is a more general position from which a specific *view / point of view* is formed.
	🖉	A(n) **alternative // different // opposing // subjective // objective** viewpoint.

19.3 Nearly but not quite right

The sentences on the left contain the types of mistakes people make when using words from this section. The correct versions are given on the right.

	Incorrect	Correct
1	The director was <u>intransigent with</u> the issue of a productivity bonus.	The director was <u>intransigent on</u> the issue of a productivity bonus.
2	The data is <u>regarded for</u> evidence of a new sub-atomic particle.	The data is <u>regarded as</u> evidence of a new sub-atomic particle.
3	There are several <u>disagreements</u> as to what constitutes an offence.	There are several different <u>opinions / views / points of view</u> as to what constitutes an offence.

	Incorrect	Correct
4	A court judge should remain <u>indifferent</u> throughout a trial.	A court judge should remain <u>impartial</u> throughout a trial.
5	The primary <u>argument to IVF of</u> some religious groups is that it uses external fertilisation.	The primary <u>objection to IVF from</u> some religious groups is that it uses external fertilisation.
6	Balkin <u>oppose</u> to sex segregation in schools as he feels it is a diversion from more important educative issues.	Balkin <u>opposes / is opposed to</u> sex segregation in schools as he feels it is a diversion from more important educative issues.
7	Many pressure groups have strong <u>views against</u> embryonic research.	Many pressure groups have strong <u>views on / about</u> embryonic research. or Many pressure groups are firmly against embryonic research.
8	Some people <u>see it as</u> since they already pay income tax, they should not be additionally taxed on interest from savings.	Some people <u>take the view that</u> since they already pay income tax, they should not be additionally taxed on interest from savings.
9	This report has outlined the factors that <u>condemn against</u> animal testing.	This report has outlined the <u>arguments against / reasons for opposing</u> animal testing.
10	The police spokesman stated that they do not <u>support</u> unprofessional behaviour by officers, or <u>condone</u> it when it happens.	The police spokesman stated that they do not <u>condone</u> unprofessional behaviour by officers, or <u>tolerate</u> it when it happens.

Cause and effect, dependency, similarity and difference

● ● ● ● ● ●

20 Cause and effect, derivation, requirement, compatibility, reciprocity and dependency

As part of analysing your material you will need to reveal the connections between things. It's important to communicate your ideas about the nature of these connections precisely (stating whether you think they are, for example, causal, reciprocal or tangential) and to give your reasons for your conclusions. A common mistake is to make a false causal connection (also called a post hoc fallacy). For example, the fact that children who play violent computer games tend to be more violent than other children does not necessarily mean that it is playing such games that causes the violent behaviour – there may be other, non-causal explanations for the correlation.

Section 20 gives you words and phrases for discussing different types of connections. I have repeatedly used one topic to help make clear which phrases are 'cause to effect' and which are 'effect to cause'. Note that different phrases need different sentence structures (take note of the commas and full stops) and/or different prepositions (for example, account **for**, have an impact **on**).

See also section 16 for influence and impact.

20.1   Words in action

Cause to effect

▸ The release of CFCs <u>causes</u> the ozone layer <u>to thin</u> / a <u>thinning of</u> the ozone layer.
▸ The release of CFCs has the <u>effect</u> of thinning of the ozone layer.
▸ The release of CFCs <u>affects</u> the ozone layer, <u>causing</u> it to thin.
▸ The release of CFCs <u>triggers</u> <u>a reaction that</u> thins the ozone layer.
▸ <u>Owing to / Because of / As a result of / As a consequence of</u> the release of CFCs, the ozone layer is thinning.
▸ CFCs are released into the atmosphere. <u>Consequently, / As a consequence, / As a result,</u> the ozone layer is becoming thinner.

- CFCs are released into the atmosphere, <u>thereby</u> thinning the ozone layer.
- <u>There is a causal link between</u> the release of CFCs and the thinning of the ozone layer.
- One <u>outcome of</u> the release of CFCs <u>is that</u> the ozone layer <u>thins</u> / <u>is the</u> thin<u>ning of</u> the ozone layer.
- The release of CFCs <u>is an important factor in</u> // <u>contributes to</u> the thin<u>ning of</u> the ozone layer.
- An election will be held in June and <u>therefore / thus</u> parties are preparing their campaigns.
- An election will be held next year, <u>hence</u> the campaign preparations.

Effect to Cause

- The thinning of the ozone layer <u>stems from / is a consequence of / results from / is due to / is caused by / is attributable to</u> the release / the releasing of CFCs.
- The thinning of the ozone layer occurs <u>through / via</u> the release of CFCs.
- Habib's theory is that dyslexia <u>arises from</u> a disorder of linguistic functioning in the brain.

Derivation, creation and explanation

- The liquid is <u>derived from</u> // <u>created by / produced by</u> cooling the gas.
- The main ingredient for aspirin <u>comes from / originates from</u> willow bark.
- Electricity can be <u>generated from</u> biofuel. / Biofuel can <u>generate</u> electricity.
- The mis-selling of loans <u>gave rise to</u> a law suit.
- The view that religious education is a form of indoctrination <u>provokes</u> a strong reaction.
- The debate on legalised abortion often <u>arouses</u> strong personal feelings.
- Evidence suggests that exposure to diabetes in the womb <u>conveys</u> a higher risk of the child developing the disease.
- The complexity and length of the questionnaire <u>accounts for / explains</u> the low return rate.

Requirement, stipulation or entailment

- The <u>prerequisites</u> for practising law are usually a law degree, training and a legal practice certificate.
- The <u>requirements</u> for completing a PhD vary between different universities within the same country.
- Good customer relations <u>require</u> direct communication between customers and frontline staff.
- The fact that the average mark is lower than last year <u>necessitates</u> a revaluation of the course syllabus.
- The structural model <u>stipulates that</u> during depression the sufferer systematically perceives the world with a negative bias.
- Higher returns on investment <u>entail / involve</u> higher risks.

Connection and dependency

- I will discuss how stream height <u>relates to</u> stream flow.
- The salary increases are <u>contingent</u> on reaching production targets.
- Life-prolonging technology and the <u>concomitant / associated / related</u> ethical issues will be discussed.
- Currency exchange rates are <u>determined by</u> a complex interaction of various market forces.
- Nonaka explains the <u>dynamic</u> process in which new knowledge is used, becoming the basis of further new knowledge.
- Recent research suggests that <u>there is a (close) link between</u> passive smoking and hearing loss.
- There is a <u>significant / strong / close // direct // positive // negative correlation between</u> advertising and reputation.
- The rise in global temperature is causing a <u>corresponding</u> rise in the amount of radiation penetrating the atmosphere.
- The physical environment <u>is essential to</u> humans.
- Humans <u>are dependent on</u> the physical environment.
- Humans and the physical environment are <u>interdependent / mutually dependent // interrelated / interconnected</u>.
- Harter (2000) claims that there is an <u>inextricable link between</u> physical appearance and self-esteem.

Compatibility and reciprocity

- Tourism can be <u>compatible</u> with environmental sustainability if carefully managed.
- The pursuit of profit is <u>incompatible / not compatible</u> with ethical modes of conduct.
- There is increasing interest in the <u>reciprocal</u> relationship between humans and their environment.

Reverse relationship

- As the supply of a currency increases, it loses value, and the <u>converse</u> is also true.
- The students in group A were asked to ignore the students in group B and <u>vice versa</u>.

20.2   Information to help you use these words correctly

affect v	=	To make a difference to or to influence something.
	≠	*Affect* and *effect*. See below.
	∗	The opposite of *affected* is *unaffected*. *Disaffected* has a different meaning, i.e. unhappy with those in authority.

arouse v **arousal** n	= v – To cause a person / people to give an emotional response. 🖉 To arouse (feelings of) **interest** // **curiosity** // **anger** // **jealousy** // **suspicion** // **sympathy**.
concomitant adj / n	= adj – (1) Naturally occurring or connected with. (2) Concurrent (happening at the same time).
contingent adj / n	= adj – (1) Conditional, dependent on future events. (2) Happening by chance. (3) In philosophy, true only under certain conditions, namely those of the truth values that make up the proposition. (4) A representative group or portion. E.g. (Of soldiers) a contingent force. ∗ A contingency is a possible future event, or plan for such an event.
converse n **conversely** adv	= n – Used to describe when elements are reversible or interchangeable. Similar to *vice versa*. ≠ *Converse* and *opposite* A converse relationship is when the different parts of the argument are interchangeable, for example, the converse of 'All Ys are Xs' is 'All Xs are Ys'. This is not the same as an opposite relationship, in which the terms are incompatible, sharing no common ground. Examples of opposites are 'long and short' and 'black and white'. ≠ *Conversely*, *in contrast* and *however* *Conversely* is used only to describe when elements are interchangeable. *In contrast* and *however* are used to introduce differences or opposites.
convey v	= (1) To communicate an idea or feeling. (2) To transport or carry. 🖉 To convey (**an**) **emotion** // **feelings** // **an idea** // **information** // **a sense of** X.
correlation n **correlate** v	= n – An interdependent link or relationship. In statistics, a correlation is where if one thing increases / decreases, the other also increases / decreases. Importantly, a correlation does not necessarily mean that one change directly causes the other. 🖉 A **strong** // **direct** // **significant** // **high** // **positive** // **negative** // **weak** correlation.

correspond v **corresponding** adj **correspondingly** adv	= v – (1) To have a directly matching relationship or link. (2) To communicate in writing with someone. ≠ *Correspondingly* and *similarly* *Correspondingly* means having a linked or matching relationship to something else. E.g. The global oil reserve is decreasing and the price of cars is rising correspondingly. Each locker number has a corresponding data entry. *Similarly* is used when one thing is done in a similar way to the other. E.g. The E9 drug will be launched at a conference in the US next May, and the E7 will be similarly launched in Germany.
dependent adj	= Needing and relying on something else. ≠ *Dependent* and *dependant* A *dependant* is a child or other relative for whom another family member is responsible.
derive v	= To obtain one thing from something else. ⌔ The data are derived **mainly / largely / primarily // solely** from government sources. To derive **pleasure // satisfaction // inspiration // profit // facts // knowledge** from X.
determine v	= To control and be the deciding factor in. *Gr* Often used in the passive. E.g. The amount of available energy **is determined by** the number of calories eaten. ∗ *Determinism* is the philosophy in which events and actions are absolutely determined by the existing conditions.

due to	= Caused by / Because of. Similar in meaning to *owing to* and *on account of*.
	Gr *Due to* and *owing to*
	These are now often used interchangeably, but strictly speaking, *due to* relates to the **noun** only and *owing to* relates to the <u>whole clause</u>.
	E.g. We are not going on the **field trip**, due to bad weather. ✘ (The field trip is not caused by the bad weather.)
	<u>We are not going on the field trip</u>, owing to bad weather. ✓
	The bad weather is due to low pressure coming in from the Atlantic. ✓
dynamic adj / n	= adj – (1) A continuously changing and developing process or system, often in the context of a two-way relationship. (2) Full of ideas and/or energy.
	n – A force that causes change.
effect n / v	= n – The change or result caused by someone or something.
	v – To cause or bring about.
	Effect as a verb is not common, except for 'to effect change'/'to effect a cure'.
	≠ *Effect* and *affect*
	Effect is the noun (to have an effect on something) and *affect* is the verb (to affect something).
	℘ n – **A beneficial / a positive // the desired // a profound // a serious // an indirect // an adverse / a detrimental // a damaging // an unintended // a cumulative // an immediate // a short-term // a long-term** effect.
entail v **entailment** n	= v – (1) To be a necessary part of or result of. Similar to *necessitate*.
	(2) To logically follow. In logic, A is said to entail B if it is the case that if A is true, B must be true, and that if A is false, B must be false.
hence adv	= (1) 'For this reason' or 'as a result of this'.
	(2) 'From now on' / 'From here'. This is a formal and somewhat old-fashioned use of *hence*. E.g. 100 years hence, the war will be forgotten.
	≠ *Hence*, *thus* and *therefore*
	Hence can often be interchanged with *thus* or *therefore*. However, *hence* is much less commonly used and usually only to talk about the present or future rather than the past. Another difference is that *hence* is followed by a noun.
	E.g. I did not go to school hence <u>my ignorance</u> about literature.
	I did not go to school therefore / thus <u>I am ignorant</u> about literature.

inextricable adj **inextricably** adv	= adj – Impossible to separate. ⌀ adv – X and Y are inextricably **linked**.
interdependent adj **interdependence** n	= Two or more things being dependent on each other. * *Co-dependent* has a similar meaning but also has the different, separate meaning of being passively and overly dependent on someone else.
mutual adj **mutually** adv **mutuality** n	= adj – Done to each other or experienced in the same way by both parties.
owing to adj phrase	= On account of / Because of. Similar in meaning to *due to*. See above for the grammatical difference between *owing to* and *due to*.
prerequisite n	= Required as a condition before something else can happen. Similar to *precondition*.
provoke v	= (1) To cause to have an action, reaction or response. Often used in science to describe biological responses. (2) To deliberately anger or annoy. ⌀ To provoke a **debate** // **a discussion** // **a controversy** // **a crisis** // **questions** // **a protest** // **an attack** // **violence** // **a response** // **a reaction.** ≠ *Provoke* and *evoke* To evoke is to cause to bring to mind a particular emotion or memory. E.g. The poem evokes memories of childhood.
reciprocal adj **reciprocity** n	= adj – Having mutual exchange and benefit between two things or groups. * A reciprocal relationship is not necessarily the same as an interdependent relationship. Two things can have a reciprocal relationship but not depend on each other.
relate to v	= To be concerned with or connected to.

stipulate v **stipulation** n	= v – To specify, require, demand, or necessitate. See also section 8, page 53. ⌀ The **model** // **regulations** // **rules** // **law** // **contract** // **instructions** // **standards** // **doctrine** // **policy** stipulate(s) that ...
thereby adv	= 'By that means' or 'as a result of that'. Gr X happens, thereby do**ing** / caus**ing** Y.
therefore adv	= For that reason, consequently.
thus adv	(1) 'By this means'. E.g. We heated the liquid, thus creating vapour. (2) 'In this way'. E.g. Presented thus, the argument is unclear. (3) 'As a result of this' / 'therefore'. E.g. The bid was successful and thus they were awarded the funds. (4) 'To this point / extent'. E.g. Thus far we have looked only at the national data. ≠ *Thus, thereby, therefore* As indicated in the examples above, meaning (1) of *thus* is similar to *thereby*, and meaning (3) is similar to *therefore*. *Thereby* means 'by that means' and *therefore* is used in the logic of argument or process. E.g. Yin published his results, thereby sharing his findings with the rest of the scientific community. ✓ Yin's results have never been replicated and I suggest that his research is thereby flawed. ✗ Yin's results have never been replicated and I suggest that his research is therefore flawed. ✓
trigger v	= To make something happen, usually suddenly. ⌀ To trigger **a crisis** // **an attack** // **a response** // **a memory** // **a collapse** // **an explosion** // **a feeling of** X.
vice versa adv	= (With the two items mentioned previously) the other way round / in reverse order. Similar to *conversely*. ✱ The spelling is *vice versa* not *visa versa*.

20.3 Nearly but not quite right

The sentences on the left contain the types of mistakes people make when using words from this section. The correct versions are given on the right.

	Incorrect	Correct
1	The average reproduction time for bacteria A was 17 minutes. <u>Conversely</u>, the average time for bacteria B was 19.2 minutes.	The average reproduction time for bacteria A was 17 minutes. <u>In contrast / However</u>, the average time for bacteria B was 19.2 minutes.
2	Deoxygenated blood is pumped from the heart into the lungs and <u>vice versa</u>.	Deoxygenated blood is pumped from the heart into the lungs, and <u>then the oxygenated blood flows back to the heart</u>.(Deoxygenated blood is not pumped back from the lungs into the heart.)
3	Testing on animals <u>influences</u> them in several <u>aspects</u>.	Testing on animals <u>affects</u> them in several <u>ways</u>.
4	Unregulated tourism can <u>cause</u> environmental and socio-cultural threats.	Unregulated tourism can <u>pose / present</u> environmental and socio-cultural threats. or Unregulated tourism can be an environmental and socio-cultural threat.
5	Noise <u>contributed by</u> road works can cause stress among residents.	Noise <u>caused</u> by road works can cause stress among residents.
6	Oxygen corrodes iron, <u>thereby it creating</u> rust.	Oxygen corrodes iron, <u>thereby / thus</u> creating rust.
7	People do not realise that the UK is also greatly <u>impacted by</u> the issue.	People do not realise that the UK is also greatly <u>affected by</u> the issue.
8	Computer games <u>have affected</u> obesity in children.	Computer games <u>have led to an increase in / have contributed to</u> obesity in children.
9	This legislation will have a <u>higher effect</u> on public transport than on car ownership.	This legislation will have a <u>greater effect</u> on public transport than on car ownership.
10	Many UK universities have <u>reciprocity</u> relationships with overseas institutions.	Many UK universities have <u>reciprocal</u> relationships with overseas institutions.

21 Equivalence, similarity, difference and diversity

This section gives you words and phrases for comparing and contrasting ideas and information – an essential part of critical analysis and argument. Importantly, you should make comparisons only if they are relevant to your point and give some type of insight into the issue you are discussing.

To compare means to examine both the similarities and differences between two or more things, and *to contrast* means to concentrate more on the differences. Remember that you must give your reasons for thinking things are similar or different, including if you use analogy. For example, if you say that the global economy is like a finely balanced ecosystem, you must explain <u>why</u> you think the one resembles the other.

See also section 19 (points of view) and section 23 (comparing the views of different authors).

21.1 Words in action

Using the words *compare* and *contrast*

▸ This assignment <u>compares</u> the birth rate of different EU member states.
▸ We conducted a quantitative <u>comparison of</u> the three habitats.
▸ We <u>compared</u> first years <u>with</u> final year students and found significant differences in analytical skills.
▸ It is incorrect to <u>compare</u> Buddhism <u>to</u> mainstream religions such as Christianity.
▸ Our <u>comparative</u> analysis shows little difference in ethical behaviour between small and large businesses.
▸ We <u>compared and contrasted</u> the two methods and found that both were equally effective.

Equivalence

▸ People often tend to <u>equate</u> knowledge <u>with</u> intelligence.
▸ I will argue that all EU member states should have <u>equal / the same</u> status.
▸ The usual method for assessing <u>parity between</u> countries is to compare the price of a 'standard' good.
▸ Each colour in Figure 1 <u>corresponds to</u> a particular country, as explained underneath the chart.
▸ The new national minimum wage rate <u>represents</u> an increase of 2.5% on the previous rate.
▸ Over 95% of human genes have a <u>counterpart</u> in the mouse genome.
▸ McMahon (1999) asks whether action research and reflective practice are <u>synonymous</u>.

Similarity, uniformity and convergence

▸ There are a number of interesting <u>similarities between</u> the US and UK financial systems.
▸ The US financial system is <u>similar to that of</u> the UK <u>in one // in several // in a number of</u> <u>respect(s)</u>.

- Old English is fairly <u>similar to</u> Middle English <u>as regards / in terms of / with respect to</u> orthography.
- Rinaldi et al. found that antioxidants are <u>similarly</u> depleted in both mild cognitive impairment and Alzheimer's disease.
- Non-profit administration <u>resembles</u> private-sector management in two important ways.
- The current financial crisis <u>has parallels with</u> the problems in some other European countries.
- I will examine how far agricultural practices can realistically <u>emulate</u> natural ecosystems.
- Vaccines <u>mimic / emulate</u> the natural infection, tricking the immune system into producing antibodies.
- Rotorb (2009) <u>draws an analogy</u> between writing a novel and painting. He explains that both are …
- We ensured that each subgroup was <u>homogeneous / uniform</u> in terms of age and income.
- Van Zoonen (2004) looks at how the <u>convergence of</u> popular culture and politics can be exploited by politicians.
- The Europa press release outlines the <u>convergent</u> views on the Multiannual Financial Framework.

Difference, differentiation and divergence

Difference

- There are a number of interesting // important <u>differences between</u> the US and UK financial systems.
- The way pesticides are used in India <u>is different / differs</u> <u>from that of</u> most other countries.
- Collins' <u>view differs from that of</u> Esty <u>as to</u> the extent to which businesses are responsible for the effects of production.
- Old and Middle English <u>differ / are different</u> <u>in that</u> Old English has much more inflection.
- The languages are quite <u>dissimilar</u> at first glance, even though they share a language family.
- The study looks at pay <u>disparity / the lack of parity in</u> pay between men and women in the UK.
- Correlation does <u>not equate to (with) / is not equal to</u> causation.

Differentiation

- In traditional theology, the presence of a soul <u>differentiates / distinguishes / separates</u> humans from animals.
- Cote and Morgan <u>differentiate / make clear the difference</u> between amplification and suppression of emotions.
- We <u>discerned small differences</u> in the way the people reacted to the sculpture <u>depending on</u> its colour.
- <u>A distinction</u> needs to be <u>made / drawn // recognised</u> between size and volume.
- Previous research has <u>distinguished</u> atoms <u>by</u> their state of oxidisation.
- There are two <u>distinct / discrete</u> categories of Bengali literature.
- Demir and Nyhan (2008) evaluate the <u>dichotomy between</u> US politics and administration.

- Wolf argues that business should not be concerned with social consequences. Svensson <u>however, / on the other hand,</u> shows that business and society are mutually dependent.
- Criminal law upholds national standards of behaviour. <u>In contrast to this, / By contrast,</u> civil law protects individuals against each other.
- Type 1 diabetes is caused by autoimmune attack, <u>whereas / while</u> type 2 diabetes is often a result of poor eating habits.

Divergence

- Cognitivist and behaviourist paradigms both deal with a common process but <u>diverge</u> on the issue of memory.
- Plato and Aristotle developed <u>divergent</u> theories of knowledge.
- Collins and Esty agree that businesses should behave ethically, but <u>their views differ in terms of / they diverge on</u> the extent to which …

Degrees of similarity or difference (See also, section 10 for information on words relating to degree and size, e.g. *minimal, pronounced*.)

Small similarities or differences

- There are (only) <u>marginal // minor / slight</u> differences // similarities between …
- We found <u>virtually no / almost no</u> difference / similarity between the two groups.
- There is a <u>subtle but important</u> distinction between X and Y in that …
- Quantitative research is unable to capture the <u>nuances</u> of human behaviour and response.

Medium-sized similarities or differences

- The results of this experiment have proved <u>quite / somewhat</u> <u>similar // different</u> in that they show …
- The <u>relative</u> lack of information on the website might indicate a desire to hide its real purpose.
- The current political situation is <u>relatively / comparatively</u> unstable compared with ten years ago.

Large similarities or differences

- <u>Considerably</u> <u>less / more</u> research has been conducted in this area of medicine <u>than</u> in any other.
- <u>Compared with</u> South East Asia, Australia has <u>considerably more // fewer</u> immigrants.
- The study indicates that there are <u>far more // far fewer</u> convictions when cases are heard without a jury.
- There are three <u>striking // obvious // notable // substantial / major / marked / pronounced</u> similarities // differences between the two theories.
- Capitalism and socialism have <u>radically / fundamentally</u> <u>different</u> approaches to wealth distribution.

Diversity

▸ There are <u>diverse / varied / different</u> opinions as to whether ethics have a valid place in a business.

▸ Ethnicity tends to be more <u>diverse</u> in larger towns and cities than in rural areas.

▸ The chemicals have <u>disparate</u> properties.

▸ Bowles (2004) argues that cooperation is of evolutionary benefit to <u>heterogeneous</u> populations.

▸ You need to present a <u>varied</u> portfolio of work in order to gain the art award.

▸ Research has shown that <u>a variety of / various</u> gene mutations are responsible for Parkinsonism.

▸ There <u>is</u> significant <u>variation</u> in the voters' opinions.

▸ The standard of the lectures in the series was <u>variable</u>.

21.2   Information to help you use these words correctly

analogy n **analogous** adj	= n – A reasoned and explained comparison between two things to show their similarities.
	✐ To **make / draw / use** an analogy. An **apt** // **good** // **close** // **helpful** // **interesting** // **crude** // **poor** // **inappropriate** // **false** analogy.
	≠ *Analogy, metaphor* and *simile*. (See also section 17, page 107.) A metaphor is the use of the image of one thing to represent another. E.g. He is a lion stalking its prey in the urban jungle. A simile also uses images to compare things but uses *like* or *as* (and so is often less powerful than a metaphor). E.g. He is **like** a lion stalking its prey. My love is **as** deep **as** the ocean.
	✷ A false analogy is a common reasoning flaw, where a comparison between objects or ideas is used to come to a conclusion that is not supported by the comparison. E.g. Dogs are like children – they love their owners in the way children love their parents.

comparative adj **comparatively** adv	= adj / adv – As judged/measured in relation to other things. When used more loosely, *comparatively* has a similar meaning to *relatively*. E.g. It is a comparatively/relatively big firm. ∂ A comparative **(dis)advantage**. A comparative **analysis** // **report** // **survey**. ≠ *Comparative* and *comparable* These words have different meanings. See *comparable* below.
compare v **comparable** adj	= v – To note the similarities and differences between things. adj – Similar or equivalent. E.g. Teachers' salaries are comparable to those of nurses. Gr *Compare* is used with **to** or **with**. Strictly speaking, *compare* **to** highlights similarities and *compare* **with** highlights differences. E.g. A software virus is often compared to a biological one. Compared with last year's figures, this year's have seen a significant rise. ✻ *Incomparable* has two meanings – (1) unable to be compared, and (2) unable to be compared because of being the best. E.g. She has an incomparable intellect.
converge v **convergence** n **convergent** adj	= v – To come together (or to start to come together) from different directions / viewpoints.
correspond v **corresponding** adj **correspondingly** adv	= v – (1) To have a directly matching relationship or link. E.g. Each number corresponds to a particular colour. (2) To communicate in writing with someone. ≠ *Correspondingly* and *similarly*. See below.
counterpart n	= A corresponding thing or person, often with the same or similar function.
dichotomy n	= A division or absolute contrast between two things.
differentiate v **differentiation** n	= v – To recognise or identify (or think you have identified) a difference between things. Similar to *distinguish* and *make a distinction*. Gr X **differentiates** A **from** B. To **differentiate between** X and Y.

discrete adj	= Separate. Similar to *distinct*.
	≠ *Discrete* and *discreet* *Discreet* means to be careful, polite and/or secretive. E.g. The website arranges 'discreet relationships' for married people. Confusingly perhaps, one meaning of the noun *discretion* (with one 'e') is the quality of being discreet.
	* *Discrete* is commonly used in maths. In other contexts *distinct* is usually used.
disparate adj	= Very different and/or fundamentally different and therefore unable to be compared.
	≠ *Disparate* and *desperate* These two words have very different meanings.
disparity n	= A significant difference.
	* Note that unlike the adjective *disparate*, a *disparity* is a difference between things that also have some similarities and can therefore be compared. For *discrepancy*, see section 9, page 57.
distinction n **distinct** adj	= n – A difference. E.g. There is a distinction between relative and absolute poverty. adj – (1) Recognisable as separate. Often used in the context of the senses. E.g. Relative and absolute poverty are distinct. A distinct smell. (2) Noticeable. E.g. There is a distinct absence of evidence in the report.
	∂ To **make / draw / recognise // clarify // maintain** a/the distinction between X and Y. A **clear // important // fundamental** distinction.
	≠ *Distinct* and *distinctive* *Distinctive* is used to describe something or someone that is unusual and/or unique because of its differences. E.g. The building has a distinctive design.

distinguish v	= To recognise a difference between things. Similar to *differentiate* and *make a distinction*. E.g. In our report we have distinguished between relative and absolute poverty. ✳ The adjective *distinguished* has a different meaning. It is used to describe someone who looks/is dignified and commands respect. E.g. She is a distinguished actress.
diverge v **divergence** n **divergent** adj	= v – To go (or to start to go) in different directions. Usually used to describe things that start from a similar point but that then separate, or to describe things that have both similarities and differences.
emulate v	= (1) To act in the same or a similar way to something or someone else. Similar to *mimic*. Often used in a bioscience context. (2) To copy something or someone in an attempt to be as good as or better than it/them.
fewer comp / det	𝒢𝓇 *Fewer* is used with plural, countable nouns. E.g. Fewer research studies.
heterogeneous adj **heterogeneity** n	= adj – (1) Having elements that are all different. Similar to *diverse*. (2) Of different types. ✳ Note the fourth 'e' – heterog**e**neous.
homogeneous adj **homogeneity** n	= adj – (1) Having elements that are all the same or similar. (2) Of the same type. ✳ *Homogeneous* also has more specialised meanings in economics, chemistry and maths.
less comp / det	𝒢𝓇 *Less* is used with **un**countable nouns. E.g. Less research.
marginal adj **marginalise** v **marginally** adv **marginalisation** n	= adj – (1) A very small amount. (2) Not important, minor or excluded. E.g. A marginal political faction. (See also section 13, page 81.) (3) Unclear or disputed. E.g. A marginal territory. ✳ *Marginal* also has other technical meanings, e.g. a marginal tax, a marginal donor.

notable n	= Interesting and important. (See also section 9, page 55.)
	✎ A notable **exception** // **absence** // **difference** // **omission**. A notable **achievement** // **accomplishment** // **success** // **contribution** // **example** // **feature**.
	≠ *Notable* and *noticeable* *Noticeable* means 'easily seen'. Something that is noticeable might not be interesting or important (notable) and something that is notable might not be easily seen.
parallel n / adj	= n – A similarity. E.g. There are many parallels between the invention of printing and of e-books. adj – (1) Side by side or at the same time. E.g. Parallel computing. (2) In geometry, two lines or surfaces having the same distance continuously between them.
	✎ To **draw** // **note** // **reveal** // **suggest** a parallel **with X** / a parallel **between X and Y**. An **obvious** // **striking** parallel.
parity n	= Equality or equivalence, usually relating to status, pay or functionality.
relative adj **relatively** adv	= adj – (1) Having more or less of a particular quality compared with something else or other things. (2) Not absolute. E.g. Wealth is a relative concept.
	✎ Relative **abundance** // **importance** // **merits** / **strengths**. Relative **decline** // **poverty** // **deprivation** // **risk** // **isolation** // **obscurity**. Relatively **easy** / **simple** / **straightforward** /**calm** / **short** / **cheap**.
similarly adv **similar** adj	= adv – In a similar way.
	≠ *Similarly* and *correspondingly* *Similarly* means in a similar way, whereas *correspondingly* means having a directly linked or matching relationship to something else. E.g. The E9 drug will be launched at a conference in the US next May, and the E7 will be similarly launched in France. The global oil reserve is decreasing and the price of cars is rising correspondingly. See also section 20, page 129.

subtle adj **subtlety** n **subtly** adv	=	adj – Small or delicate so as to be difficult to see, recognise or describe. A subtle **difference** // **distinction** // **shift** // **variation** // **improvement** // **effect** // **influence**.
synonymous adj	=	(1) (Of words) Having the same meaning. (2) The same as, very similar or closely connected to.
	Gr	X is synonymous **with** Y.
variable adj	=	(1) Changeable. E.g. A variable interest rate. (2) Inconsistent and therefore not good. E.g. Safety standards at the factory were variable.
varied adj	=	Having differences / diversity (variety) within it. E.g. A varied diet is necessary for good health. The members of the group have varied interests.
variety n **various** adj	=	n – (1) A (large) group or collection of things or occasions that are different. Similar to *range of*. E.g. You need to eat a variety of vegetables to maintain health. (2) A type of. E.g. Supermarkets sell only a few of the many existing varieties of apple. adj – Several or many different types of something. E.g. We used various techniques in our experiment.
vary v	=	To make different or to change something. E.g. We varied the temperature according to the different melting points of each solid.

21.3 Nearly but not quite right

The sentences on the left contain the types of mistakes people make when using words from this section. The correct versions are given on the right.

	Incorrect	Correct
1	There <u>is a variety of</u> main blood groups.	There are four main blood groups.
2	Cote and Morgan <u>make a difference</u> between amplification and suppression of emotions.	Cote and Morgan <u>differentiate</u> between amplification and suppression of emotions.

	Incorrect	Correct
3	Traditional medical intervention has <u>less</u> benefits compared with alternative treatments.	Traditional medical intervention has <u>fewer</u> benefits compared with alternative treatments.
4	I suggest that a <u>parallel</u> can be <u>made</u> between the current global financial downturn and the depression in the 1930s.	I suggest that a <u>parallel</u> can be <u>drawn</u> between the current global financial downturn and the depression in the 1930s.
5	New York has an extremely <u>various</u> population.	New York has an extremely <u>varied / diverse</u> population.
6	Sierra Leone is a <u>relative</u> small country.	Sierra Leone is a <u>relatively</u> small country.
7	We found a <u>distinctive</u> difference of 8.4 grams between the 'before' and 'after' weights.	We found a <u>distinct</u> difference of 8.4 grams between the 'before' and 'after' weights.
8	DNA <u>differentiates</u> from RNA in that it is a double helix as opposed to a single-chained structure.	DNA <u>differs</u> from RNA in that it is a double helix as opposed to a single-chained structure.
9	As the company had a somewhat <u>varied</u> safety record, their franchise was not renewed.	As the company had a somewhat <u>variable</u> safety record, their franchise was not renewed.
10	My past work experience has been <u>different</u>, involving jobs in four different industries.	My past work experience has been <u>diverse</u>, involving jobs in four different industries.

Analysing and evaluating ideas

● ● ● ● ● ●

22 Analysing ideas and suggesting common themes

Analysing something involves taking it apart in order to examine it in detail, and is the first stage in what is sometimes referred to as 'synthesis'. Section 22 gives you vocabulary for analysing your material and for then starting to evaluate it by using your analysis to identify or suggest common themes and threads. (The term 'critical analysis' refers to the combination of analysis and evaluation.)

See also section 21 for the vocabulary of similarity and difference.

22.1 Words in action

Analysing concepts, ideas and arguments

▸ If we <u>break down / separate out</u> the term 'law' <u>into its constituent</u> <u>parts / components / elements</u>, we can see that …

▸ <u>Superficially, / On the surface,</u> Lok's argument is just about freedom, <u>but on closer</u> <u>examination / inspection / scrutiny</u> it is also …

▸ Simply using the 'freedom' label <u>blurs the (crucial) distinction between</u> individual and collective choice.

▸ It is a common <u>confusion to think that / misconception that</u> 'democracy' means that everyone …

▸ The paper <u>misuses</u> the term 'Web 2.0' by relating it to advances in technology rather than to how it should be used.

▸ When discussing poverty <u>we need to be clear on whether</u> we are talking about relative or absolute poverty.

▸ It is important to <u>recognise / acknowledge / realise</u> that some resources are more natural than others.

▸ In order to asses Froom's argument we first need to <u>unpick / deconstruct</u> the way he uses the concept of feminism.

▸ <u>Separating / Uncoupling / Dissociating</u> rights from responsibilities gives us a clearer picture of the issue.

▸ <u>A distinction</u> needs to be <u>made / drawn</u> between rate, speed and velocity.

- Bengali literature is <u>not homogeneous</u>; it has two <u>distinct / discrete</u> categories. West Bengali literature …
- The chemicals all have <u>disparate</u> properties.
- Correlation <u>does not equal / is not the same thing as / is not synonymous with</u> causation.
- The idea of intelligent design can be <u>traced back to</u> Thomas Aquinas in the 13th century.

Revealing or discovering common assumptions, themes or characteristics (See also sections 21 and 23 for useful vocabulary.)

- This analysis of the studies <u>reveals</u> the general underlying premise that ethical business behaviour is desirable.
- The <u>common theme</u> <u>that emerges from / emerging from</u> both arguments is that there is a lack of political will …
- A <u>common / shared</u> <u>idea / theme</u> in the articles is a questioning of the perceived benefits of student autonomy.
- A <u>thread running through</u> the articles is a questioning of the perceived benefits of student autonomy.
- <u>What makes these arguments interesting is that they all agree</u> that patients are being harmed by online advice.
- <u>The conclusion common to</u> the studies is that the demand for organ transplants can never be met purely by donation.
- There are a number of interesting <u>similarities between</u> the three studies.
- Deconstructionism looks at what is created via the text in the reader's mind and <u>similarly</u>, reader-response deals with text-to-reader transmission.
- Non-profit administration <u>resembles</u> private-sector management in two important ways.
- The current financial crisis in the UK <u>has parallels with</u> the problems in some other European countries.

22.2 Information to help you use these words correctly

analyse v analysis n	=	v – To break something down into its basic elements in order to examine and reveal its important characteristics and/or meaning.
	≠	*Analyse, analysis* and *analyses* (US spellings are *analyze, analysis* and *analyses*) These are all the same root word but the different spellings can be confusing. *To analyse* is the verb (e.g. I will analyse the data) and analy**sis** is the noun (e.g. We need to do an analysis). Analy**ses** is both the third person singular of the verb (e.g. He analyses the results regularly) and the plural noun (e.g. I compared the two analyses).

constituent adj / n	= n – (1) An element or component within a whole. (2) In politics, a member of a constituency. adj – Individual and/or separate within a whole.
deconstruct v **deconstruction** n	= v – To break something down into its component parts for the purpose of analysis. Used mainly in the fields of literature, linguistics and philosophy. * The words *dismantle* and *disassemble* have similar meanings but are less appropriate for academic writing. For *construct* see section 18, page 112.
discrete adj	= Separate. Similar to *distinct*. (See also section 21, page 139.) * *Discrete* is commonly used in maths. In other contexts *distinct* is usually used. ≠ *Discrete* and *discreet* *Discreet* means to be careful, polite and/or secretive. E.g. The website arranges 'discreet relationships' for married people.
disparate adj	= Very and/or fundamentally different and therefore unable to be compared. (See also section 21, page 139.)
dissociate v **dissociation** n	= v – (1) To separate from. (2) To stop meeting / associating with. * *Dissociate* and *disassociate* These two words have the same meaning, dis**soc**iate being the more correct.
distinct adj **distinction** n	= adj – (1) Recognisable as separate. Often used in the context of the senses. E.g. Relative and absolute poverty are distinct. A distinct smell. (2) Noticeable. E.g. There is a distinct absence of evidence in the report. ≠ *Distinct* and *distinctive* *Distinctive* is used to describe something or someone that is unusual and/or unique because of its differences. E.g. The building has a distinctive design. (See also section 21, page 139.)
emerge v **emergence** n	= v – To gradually become apparent or to gradually develop. (See also section 1, page 1.)

heterogeneous adj **heterogeneity** n	= adj – (1) Having elements that are all different. Similar to *diverse*. (2) Of different types. ∗ Note the fourth 'e' – heterogen**e**ous.
homogeneous adj **homogeneity** n	= adj – (1) Having elements that are all the same or similar. (2) Of the same type. ∗ *Homogeneous* also has more specialised meanings in economics, chemistry and maths.
misconceive v **misconception** n	= v – (1) To plan or judge something poorly or incorrectly. (2) To misunderstand. n – An incorrect belief or opinion. (See also section 18, page 113.)
parallel n / adj	= n – A similarity. adj – (1) Side by side or at the same time. E.g. Parallel computing. (2) In geometry, two lines or surfaces having the same distance continuously between them. ✐ To **draw** // **note** // **reveal** // **suggest** a parallel **with X** / a parallel **between X and Y**. An **obvious** // **striking** parallel.
reveal v	= To allow or cause something to be recognised or seen. ∗ You can only reveal something that was already there. In academic writing we usually say 'the data / experiment / analysis … revealed …' rather than ' I revealed …'.
scrutiny n **scrutinise** v	= n – Careful examination. ✐ **Careful** / **close** / **thorough** / **rigorous** scrutiny. To **come under** / **undergo** / **be subjected to** // **face** scrutiny.
superficial adj **superficially** adv	= adj – (1) Existing or happening only on the surface. (2) Lacking authenticity or real / deep understanding. ✐ Superficial **understanding** // **knowledge** // **change** // **difference** // **similarity** // **treatment** // **level** // **way**.

synonymous adj	=	(1) (Of words) Having the same meaning. (See also section 21.) (2) The same as, very similar or closely connected to.
	Gr	X is synonymous **with** Y.
theme n	=	The main topic or idea.
thread v / n	=	n – (1) A particular point or aspect within a general theme / topic that runs through all the different parts or stages of one or more books, essays, plays, arguments etc. (2) A long strand of cotton, nylon or other material.
	∂	(A) **common** // **unbroken** // **unifying** // **different** / **disparate** thread(s).
uncouple v **uncoupling** n	=	v – To separate or disconnect one thing from another / others.
	*	The word *uncouple* has a similar meaning but is used mainly in the contexts of electronics, machinery and vehicles.

22.3   Nearly but not quite right

The sentences on the left contain the types of mistakes people make when using words from this section. The correct versions are given on the right.

	Incorrect	Correct
1	Our analysis <u>discovered</u> several fundamental flaws in her argument.	Our analysis <u>revealed</u> several fundamental flaws in her argument.
2	First, let's clarify <u>if</u> ID cards will really deter terrorists <u>or not</u>.	First, let's clarify <u>whether</u> ID cards will really deter terrorists.
3	<u>Separating</u> the concept of liberal democracy <u>or</u> direct democracy is crucial because …	<u>Separating</u> the concept of liberal democracy <u>from / and</u> direct democracy is crucial because …
4	In order to analyse the problem we first need to <u>have a distinction</u> between public and private law.	In order to analyse the problem we first need to <u>draw a distinction / make a distinction / distinguish</u> between public and private law.

	Incorrect	Correct
5	No group of students can be completely <u>homogenous</u>, even if composed of only two students.	No group of students can be completely <u>homogeneous</u>, even if composed of only two students.
6	There are four chemical substances involved, each of which plays a different role in the process. These <u>desperate</u> elements are …	There are four chemical substances involved, each of which plays a different role in the process. These <u>disparate</u> elements are …
7	The <u>thread</u> of Perdue and Gurtman's study (1990) is unconscious ageism.	The <u>theme / topic</u> of Perdue and Gurtman's study (1990) is unconscious ageism.
8	The emergence <u>in</u> graffiti as a recognised art form started in New York.	The emergence <u>of</u> graffiti as a recognised art form started in New York.
9	An underlying assumption shared by both studies <u>are</u> that poor eating habits can be changed relatively easily.	An underlying assumption shared by both studies <u>is</u> that poor eating habits can be changed relatively easily.
10	Oswald (1999) showed clearly that wealth is not synonymous <u>to</u> happiness.	Oswald (1999) showed clearly that wealth is not synonymous <u>with</u> happiness.

23 Comparing the views of different authors and describing how they cite and evaluate each other

In your evaluation of sources you need to show that you understand what the authors are doing (or trying to do), where they position themselves in relation to your issue, and how these positions relate to your own.

To describe what an author is doing (without necessarily saying whether you agree or disagree with them) you need to be precise in your use of reporting verbs such as *argue, discuss, examine, explain, give, state, suggest, trace, question*. Each verb has a different meaning and it is important to show your reader that you understand what the source is doing by using an appropriate reporting verb.

E.g. Mepham (2006) <u>questions</u> the method of 'learning' bioethics and <u>states</u> that a critical approach is fundamental to the field.

The research findings of Lobstein et al. <u>justify</u> their recommendation to use the traffic-light system of food labelling.

To describe the position an author takes you can use the words and phrases given in section 19 (points of view). It is important to show your reader that you have correctly identified the position an author takes in relation to your topic or issue.

E.g. Booles is an <u>advocate of / supporter of //</u> <u>opponent of</u> stem cell research.

Taleb's <u>view is that</u> some traditional mathematical concepts can be limiting.

Section 23 gives you words and phrases for comparing and contrasting the views of different authors. See also section 21 (similarity and difference) and section 19 (points of view).

23.1 Words in action

Similar and convergent views

▸ <u>Both</u> Marteinson <u>and</u> Bergson view humour as arising from conflict between the real and the unreal.

▸ Cote and Morgan <u>are in agreement with / agree with / share the same view as / hold a similar view to</u> Hochschild, that is, that supressing emotions can cause stress in employees.

▸ Cote and Morgan, <u>together with</u> Hochschild, hold the view that supressing emotions can cause stress in workers.

▸ <u>Neither</u> Wolf <u>nor</u> Carr feels that businesses should concern themselves with ethics.

▸ Both articles show <u>considerable overlap in</u> how they view the link between literacy and reasoning.

▸ There is <u>overlap between / common ground between</u> the two authors, as they both view humour as arising from ...

▸ Collins' and Esty's positions <u>converge</u> on the issue of business and social responsibility.

Different and divergent views

▸ Clint and others maintain that humour is used to assert superiority. <u>However, / In contrast, / On the other hand,</u> Berlyne proposes that humour serves to relieve tension.

▸ Clint and others maintain that humour is used to assert superiority. Berlyne, <u>however, / in contrast, / on the other hand,</u> proposes that humour serves to relieve tension.

▸ <u>Whereas / Although</u> Wolf believes that businesses operate separately from society, Wood shows that the two are mutually dependent.

▸ Wolf <u>suggests that</u> businesses should operate separately from society, <u>while / whereas</u> Wood shows that they are interdependent.

▸ Wolf <u>states that</u> business should act separately from society, but <u>opponents of this view</u> believe that the two are co-dependent.

▸ There are <u>diverse / varied / different</u> opinions as to whether ethics do have a valid place in a business.

▸ The literature reveals two <u>different / distinct / discrete</u> theories.

▸ <u>Although both</u> Miller and Hurley <u>agree</u> that humour is connected to sexual selection, <u>they disagree on / their views differ in regard to / they diverge on</u> the extent of the role humour plays.

▸ Miller's <u>view differs from that of</u> Hurley <u>as to</u> the degree of importance humour has in evolutionary selection.

Describing how one source cites another as support and/or comments positively

▸ Barick et al. (2002) cite Bakan as <u>an advocate of the idea that</u> achieving status is a key goal in social interaction.

▸ Halle <u>quotes</u> from Le Corbusier (1986) <u>as support for his argument that</u> abstract art has been idealised in art theory.

▸ Hepner <u>paraphrases / uses paraphrases from // quotes from / uses quotations from</u> the Bible <u>as justification for</u> his ideas.

▸ Hepner uses Bible <u>extracts / excerpts</u> <u>(in an attempt) to defend / to justify</u> his ideas.

▸ <u>According to</u> Woolf, Austen <u>made a great contribution to</u> fiction, despite not having a private writing space.

▸ Woolf <u>acknowledged</u> Austen's contribution to fiction and the fact that she wrote despite not having any private space.

▸ Jung <u>credited</u> Gross <u>with</u> hav<u>ing</u> preceded him in identifying two distinct types of consciousness.

Describing how sources challenge and/or respond to each other

▸ <u>According to</u> Phillipson (2000), Crystal has a Eurocentric view of English as a global language.

- Crystal (2000) <u>responds to / replies to</u> Phillipson's criticism <u>by stating that</u> he merely describes how English is used.
- Svensson and Wood (2007) <u>disagree with / contest / refute</u> Friedman's claim that businesses do not need to consider social issues, and state that <u>on the contrary</u>, businesses have an enormous impact on society.
- Ainsworth <u>rejects / repudiates // contests / refutes</u> Dawkins' claim that faith schools are discriminatory, and states that <u>on the contrary</u>, such schools allow children informed choice.
- Ainsworth <u>counters / rebuts</u> Dawkins' claim that faith schools are discriminatory <u>by proposing that / with the proposition that / by maintaining that / by asserting that</u> such schools allow children informed choice.
- Guthrie and Parker (1989) offer <u>a rebuttal of</u> Legitimacy Theory. They suggest that ...
- Lupton (1998) <u>challenges / questions</u> Fox's suggestion that doctors are no longer seen as the authorities on medical issues.
- Gould <u>is (strongly / vigorously) challenged by</u> Dawkins, who accuses him of writing for 'middle of the road religious people'.
- Phillipson has <u>criticised</u> linguists such as Crystal for having a Eurocentric view of the global dominance of English.
- Watson and Crick <u>failed to credit</u> Franklin in their initial publication on the structure of DNA.

23.2 Information to help you use these words correctly

according to prep	=	'As stated by'.
	✳	Only use *according to* when referring to other people or organisations. It is incorrect to say 'According to me ...'.
acknowledge v	=	(1) To accept or admit something, or to show gratitude for something. (2) In academic writing, *to acknowledge* can mean to reference / cite an author, i.e. to give their name and details of publication.
assert v **assertion** n	=	v – (1) To state something clearly and confidently. (2) To do something that makes others recognise your authority or right(s). (See also section 24, page 159.)

cite v	= To refer to someone or something else, either by quotation, paraphrase or name only.
	✱ Use *cite* only to describe when one author mentions another. It is incorrect to say 'I cite …'.
	≠ *Cite*, *site* and *sight* Note the different spellings of these three different words.
contest n / v	= v – To argue against a statement. Similar to *refute* and *rebut*.
	✐ To contest the **claim** // **suggestion** // **accusation** // **idea** // **theory** that …
	✱ The verb is pronounced con<u>test</u> and the noun is pronounced <u>con</u>test.
converge v **convergence** n **convergent** adj	= v – To come together (or to start to come together) from different directions / points.
counter v	= To respond with an opposing argument, view or action. (See also section 26, pages 173 and 177.)
	✐ To counter **a claim** // **an argument** // **a threat** // **a criticism** // **fundamentalism** // **terrorism** // **extremism**.
	✱ To say that '**X is counter to** Y' or '**X runs counter to** Y' has the slightly different meaning of an action that purposely or perhaps accidentally goes against something else. E.g. Building on this site would run counter to the government's policy of maintaining green spaces. For *counterargument* see section 26, page 177.
diverge v **divergence** n **divergent** adj	= v – To go (or to start to go) in different directions. Usually used to describe things that start from a similar point but that then separate, or to describe things that have some similarities but also some differences.

excerpt n	= A short section from a book, film or piece of music. Similar to an *extract*.
	≠ *Excerpt* and *exert* These two words sound the same but have different spellings and meanings. *To exert* means to put pressure on someone or to make an effort to do something.
extract n / v	= n – A short section from a book, film or piece of music. Similar to an *excerpt*. v – To take or get something out of something else often with the use of force. E.g. We extracted DNA from each cell.
	* The noun is pronounced <u>ex</u>tract and the verb is pronounced ext<u>ract</u>.
justify v **justification** n	= v – To give or show your reasons or evidence.
	ℰ To justify **a(n) action** // **act** // **choice** // **decision** // **assertion** // **claim** // **argument** // **position** // **point of view**. To **try** // **attempt** // **seek** to justify.
maintain v	= *Maintain* has several different meanings. In the context of evaluating sources, it means to state something clearly and confidently (with or without evidence), often in the face of criticism. Similar to *claim*. (See also sections 24 and 25.)
paraphrase v / n	= v – To express the meaning of writing or speech using different words, often in order to clarify or simplify.
quote v **quotation** n	= v – To use the exact words of someone else.
	≠ *quote / quotation* and *cite / citation* *Citation* is sometimes used to mean *quotation*. However, a citation can also refer to any type of reference to a source, including paraphrase or just giving the name of the author.
	* It is incorrect to say 'I quote that …' or 'Smith quotes that …' to introduce a quotation. *Quote* is usually only used to describe when one source quotes another. E.g. Smith quotes Robinson: 'Job satisfaction is …'.
rebut v **rebuttal** n	= v – To argue against a statement. Similar to *contest* and *refute* but less commonly used.

refute v	$=$ v – To oppose a statement and, importantly, to try to prove that the statement is false. Similar to *contest and rebut*.
refutation n	
	🔗 To refute the **claim** // **suggestion** // **accusation** // **idea** // **theory** that ...
reject v	$=$ v – To not accept.
rejection n	
	$\neq$ *Reject*, *refute* and *deny*
	Reject has the more general meaning.
	To *refute* is a more formal word used only in the context of argument and ideas. It differs from both *reject* and *deny* because *refute* must include giving reasons for not accepting a statement.
	To *deny* often means to reject an accusation or the truth of something, and is not usually appropriate in an academic context.
repudiate v	$=$ v – To strongly reject, deny or refuse to accept the truth or validity of something. Similar to *reject* but more formal.
repudiation n	

23.3 Nearly but not quite right

The sentences on the left contain the types of mistakes people make when using words from this section. The correct versions are given on the right.

	Incorrect	Correct
1	<u>According to me</u>, the issue of global warming is not as serious as the media portrays.	<u>In my view, / I suggest that</u> the issue of global warming is not as serious as the media portrays.
2	Kerlinger (1969) <u>quotes</u> that '*Science* is a misused and misunderstood word' (p. 1127).	Kerlinger (1969) <u>states</u> that '*Science* is a misused and misunderstood word' (p. 1127).
3	It has been <u>alleged</u> that computer games can be used to educate children.	It has been <u>claimed / suggested / stated / proved</u> ... that computer games can be used to educate children.
4	Smith (2009) has criticised Ramone's work <u>as</u> being overcomplicated.	Smith (2009) has criticised Ramone's work <u>for</u> being overcomplicated.
5	Karl Marx <u>refuted</u> capitalism as a positive system for social development.	Karl Marx <u>rejected</u> capitalism as a positive system for social development.

	Incorrect	Correct
6	According to Gilchrist, <u>he suggests that</u> we need to re-evaluate how we perceive risk-taking heroines.	According to Gilchrist, we need to re-evaluate how we perceive risk-taking heroines.
7	Kroll <u>states</u> Frie as an example of an early approach to second language learning.	Kroll <u>uses // gives // cites // quotes // paraphrases</u> Frie as an example of an early approach to second language learning.
8	The research team <u>knowledge</u> that their data is incomplete and that further studies are needed.	The research team <u>acknowledges</u> that their data is incomplete and that further studies are needed.
9	According to <u>(Dr Reynolds, 2000)</u> there is no strong evidence of long-term damage to health.	According to <u>Reynolds (2000)</u> there is no strong evidence of long-term damage to health.
10	As Collins (1994) <u>cites</u> '... good ethics is synonymous with good management' (p. 2).	As Collins (1994) <u>states</u>, '... good ethics is synonymous with good management' (p. 2).

24 Evaluating an author's ideas positively

This section gives you words and phrases for introducing and giving comments on sources positively by using what I call here 'neutral' or 'positive' language. Doing this is a crucial way of evaluating your sources, making shifts in meaning, and controlling the direction of your argument. For a definition of *argument*, see section 5, page 29.

24.1   Words in action

Using neutral verbs to introduce a source and then giving a positive comment

▸ Collins <u>states // asserts // claims / maintains // contends</u> that violence is a product of environmental factors. Other studies support this idea …

▸ Darwin <u>proposed / suggested</u> that individuals are 'selected' by nature over others. This idea is now well established as …

▸ Vellitino <u>examines // considers / takes into account // covers in detail</u> the four different concepts of dyslexia. He shows that …

Using positive verbs to comment on a source

▸ Milanovic (2002) <u>explains</u> how globalisation can affect income distribution. His findings are important because …

▸ Miller (1991) <u>explicates</u> the process by which people develop mental models of relationships. He illustrates how …

▸ The authors <u>demonstrate / illustrate / show / establish</u> that well-run businesses are of benefit to society. Their findings …

▸ Thouless <u>observed / made the observation / noted</u> that homing pigeons do not need to know the sun's location in order to fly home.

▸ Skinner <u>found</u> that reinforcement strengthens patterns of behaviour.

▸ Perdue and Gurtman (1990) <u>identify</u> an important and overlooked factor in ageism, namely …

▸ Rubia investigates aspects of neuropsychology and <u>clarifies / elucidates</u> the nature of psychiatric disorders.

▸ The article successfully <u>simplifies</u> the complex theory of special relativity.

▸ Stich (1985) <u>provides</u> some illuminating examples of human irrationality. The most interesting is …

Using positive adjectives, adverbs and nouns to comment on a source

▸ Plamondon gives a <u>comprehensive / thorough // extensive</u> overview of handwriting systems and offers <u>clear // useful insights</u> into …

▸ Bergl and Vigilant provide <u>important // interesting // reliable / sound</u> data on Cross River gorilla migration. Their data …

▸ The article contains <u>overwhelming // compelling // convincing // objective // hard / strong / clear // ample</u> <u>evidence that</u> …

▸ Their research <u>conclusively // convincingly</u> <u>shows / establishes</u> that environment affects mental health.

▸ In my view, Perdue and Gurtman (1990) <u>correctly</u> identify an important and previously overlooked factor in ageism, namely …

▸ He provides a <u>cogent // coherent / logical / sound / valid // reasonable // considered</u> argument to support his theory that …

▸ Skinner puts forward <u>innovative // convincing / persuasive / plausible / credible</u> ideas about teaching methodology.

▸ Stich (1985) provides some <u>illuminating examples</u> of human irrationality. The most interesting is …

▸ The report <u>benefits from</u> <u>rigorous</u> research, a <u>succinct</u> style and a <u>readable</u> format.

▸ <u>A clear strength of</u> the survey is the very large sample size.

Stating that a source is supported by other research

▸ The idea proposed by Valencia-Flores et al. (2002) that the 'siesta culture' of Mexican students is a negative stereotype is <u>supported / corroborated / confirmed / verified / validated /substantiated</u> by other research in this area. Studies by …

▸ Importantly, the findings are <u>consistent with</u> those of previous studies.

Stating that a source has contributed to the field

▸ His <u>substantive</u> body of work has <u>influenced</u> many areas of psychology. The most important area has been …

▸ Kramer's article is a <u>noteworthy // valuable // substantive</u> <u>contribution to</u> the debate on corporate responsibility because …

24.2 Information to help you use these words correctly

assert v **assertion** n	= v – To state something clearly and confidently. (2) To do something that makes others recognise your authority or right(s).
claim v / n	= v – To state something clearly and confidently, with or without evidence. Similar to *maintain*. *Gr* v – To claim that ... n – To **make** a/the claim that ...
cogent adj	= Logical, clear and convincing. Usually used in the context of argumentation. ⌀ A cogent **argument** // **case**. To **put forward** / **propose** a cogent argument // case.
coherent adj	= Logical, well-structured and consistent. ⌀ A coherent **argument** // **article** // **framework** // **strategy** // **policy** // **system** // **theory**. To do X in a coherent **way** / **manner**. ≠ *Coherent, cogent* and *cohesive* *Coherent* and *cogent* are often used interchangeably but strictly speaking, a coherent argument is well-structured but not necessarily cogent (convincing). *Cohesive* means 'sticking together' and is usually used in the context of physical things rather than argument. E.g. They formed a cohesive group in order to survive.
comprehensive adj	= Covering all or nearly all aspects, very wide-ranging. Similar meaning to *thorough*. ⌀ (A) comprehensive **review** // **examination** // **study** // **account** // **coverage** // **survey**.
conclusive adj **conclusively** adv	= adj – (Of an argument or evidence) very strong and convincing. ⌀ X **is** / **provides** / **gives** // **shows** conclusive **proof** / **evidence** // **results**. For *inconclusive*, see section 25, page 168.

consistent adj	= (1) Does not contradict. (2) Unchanging over time.
	Gr X is consistent **with** Y.
	ℰ A consistent **approach** // **standard** // **level**. X is consistent with the **aim** // **data** // **evidence** / **findings** // **objective** // **principle** // **view** of Y.
contend v **contention** n	= v – (1) To state something to be argued, with or without evidence. Similar to *assert*. (2) To have to compete with something or face a particular difficultly.
corroborate v **corroboration** n	= v – To support something by giving additional data, evidence or information. Similar to *support* except that *corroborate* is usually used for concrete evidence or empirical data rather than ideas and theories.
credible adj	= Authoritative and convincing.
	ℰ (A) credible **source** // **evidence** // **data** // **argument** // **explanation** // **threat** // **deterrent**. **Scientifically** // **politically** // **academically** credible.
elucidate v	= To explain and clarify.
	✱ *Elucidate* is more formal than *explain* or *clarify*.
explicate v **explication** n	= v – To analyse something in detail in order to understand its meaning and significance.
	≠ *Explicate* and *explain* These words have different meanings. *To explicate* means to analyse (break down and explore) something at a deep level. E.g. The third paragraph of this explication looks at how the poem's rhythm adds to its meaning. *To explain* means to give a description of something and/or to give the reasons why something happens or exists. E.g. The appendix gives an explanation of the different categories of hospital.

extensive adj	= (1) Covering many aspects of an issue or idea. E.g. an extensive survey. (2) Covering a wide area.
	≠ *Extensive* and *expansive* *Expansive* also means wide ranging but is used in the context of physical space (e.g. an expansive area). It also means the personal characteristic of being very communicative.
	≠ *Extensive* and *comprehensive* *Extensive* means covering many aspects, whereas *comprehensive* means covering all or nearly all aspects. For *expand* see section 11, page 70.
illuminate v **illuminating** adj	= v – (1) To clarify, providing understanding and insight. (2) To provide light.
	ℰ An illuminating **example** // **discussion** // **piece of research** // **lecture** // **experience**. For *insight*, see section 18, page 113.
illustrate v **illustration** n	= v – (1) To give an example and/or to demonstrate. (2) To use / provide with pictures.
	ℰ To illustrate **a point** // **an argument** // **a principle** // **a concept**. To illustrate the/a(n) **importance** // **complexity** // **difficulty** // **problem** // **concept** // **model**. X **seeks to** / **attempts to** / **tries to** // **serves to** illustrate Y.
maintain v	= *Maintain* has several different meanings. In the context of evaluating sources, *maintain* means to state something clearly and confidently (with or without evidence), often in the face of criticism. Similar to *claim*. (See also sections 23 and 25.)
noteworthy adj	= Worth special attention.
plausible adj	= (Without evidence) seeming to be reasonable and believable.
	ℰ A plausible **explanation** // **theory** // **argument** // **hypothesis** // **idea** // **interpretation**.

substantiate v	=	To provide additional supporting evidence or information. Similar to *corroborate* and *support*.
substantive adj	=	(1) Dealing with facts, issues and evidence (and therefore having real-world importance) rather than with theoretical concepts, formal logic or methodology. E.g. Phillips (1974) looks at both the substantive and theoretical implications of the suicide data. (2) Important, main.
	✎	A substantive **issue** // **body of work** // **report** // **piece of research**.
	≠	*Substantive* and *Substantial* *Substantial* means of a large size or quantity.
succinct adj	=	Brief and clear.
valid adj **validity** n	=	adj – (1) Reasonable, well-founded and supported by evidence. (2) Logically consistent, i.e. the conclusion follows from the premise. In formal logic, an argument may be valid even though its premise and/or conclusion are untrue. E.g. All birds are blue. This swan is a bird. Therefore, this swan is blue.
	✎	**Scientifically** // **statistically** // **logically** valid. A valid **argument** // **assumption** // **opinion** // **belief** // **viewpoint** // **interpretation** // **explanation**. For *invalid*, see section 25, page 169.
validate v	=	To confirm or prove.
verify v	=	To prove the truth of something.

24.3   Nearly but not quite right

The sentences on the left contain the types of mistakes people make when using words from this section. The correct versions are given on the right.

	Incorrect	Correct
1	The new company is extremely <u>innovated</u>.	The new company is extremely <u>innovative</u>.
2	The National Bureau of Economic Research has been <u>a great benefit for</u> the field of economics.	The National Bureau of Economic Research has been <u>of great benefit to</u> the field of economics.
3	I will look at both the theoretical and <u>substantial</u> implications of recent research on the consequences of job insecurity.	I will look at both the theoretical and <u>substantive</u> implications of recent research on the consequences of job insecurity.
4	Lupton <u>describes</u> that the public is interested in health news, and this idea is supported by other findings.	Lupton <u>shows / establishes / demonstrates</u> that the public is interested in health news, and this idea is supported by other findings.
5	Oswald <u>brings some insights</u> into how we can measure happiness more effectively.	Oswald <u>gives / offers us (some) insights</u> into how we can measure happiness more effectively.
6	Roger's explanation of the effect of caffeine on performance seems to me the most <u>possible</u> because …	Roger's explanation of the effect of caffeine on performance seems to me the most <u>plausible</u> because …
7	The <u>viability</u> of this belief is called into question by recent evidence.	The <u>validity</u> of this belief is called into question by recent evidence.
8	Although the survey is <u>comprehensive</u>, it fails to look at applications of learning curve theory.	Although the survey is <u>extensive / wide-ranging</u>, it fails to look at applications of learning curve theory.
9	Carr (1968) uses the <u>illustrating</u> analogy of a poker player to demonstrate his position on business ethics.	Carr (1968) uses the <u>illuminating</u> analogy of a poker player to demonstrate his position on business ethics.
10	Importantly, the findings are <u>consistent to</u> those of previous studies.	Importantly, the findings are <u>consistent with</u> those of previous studies.

25 Evaluating an author's ideas negatively

This section gives you what I call 'neutral' and 'negative' language for commenting on sources with which you disagree. An important part of evaluating your material and of developing an argument is to present opposing views, and to show why they are not as convincing as your own (a process called *rebuttal*). You will often need to give only a brief *rebuttal*, but you should always do it fairly – don't insult your reader's intelligence by not representing properly the strengths of the opposing arguments. At the end of your rebuttal it is useful to restate how your position differs from that of the opposing arguments, and vocabulary for doing this is given in sections 26 to 28.

See also section 19 (points of view) and section 26 (conceding and disagreeing) for other useful words and phrases.

25.1 Words in action

Using neutral verbs to introduce a source and then giving a negative comment

▸ Collins <u>asserts // claims / maintains // contends</u> that violence is a product of environmental factors. <u>However</u>, other studies show that …

▸ The report <u>proposes // states // suggests</u> that all students should do an internship. This is <u>not a sensible</u> policy because …

▸ Vellitino <u>examines // considers // covers</u> different concepts of dyslexia <u>but does not</u> identify the synergies between them.

Using negative forms of positive verbs to comment on a source

▸ Jones <u>does not</u> consider // show / demonstrate // establish the fact that the virus has mutated.

Using negative verbs to comment on a source

▸ Delaware <u>neglects / overlooks / omits / does not take into account // ignores</u> the fact that …
▸ The report <u>fails to</u> draw a distinction between children and adults.
▸ The study <u>complicates</u> what is in fact a relatively simple phenomenon.
▸ The report <u>suffers from</u> a lack of detailed analysis.
▸ The theory of blending inheritance was later <u>disproved / discredited</u> and superseded by the theory of …
▸ The fact that there are several digressions <u>detracts from</u> the main argument.
▸ The diagrams and tables <u>distract</u> (the reader) <u>from</u> the main point of the text.
▸ Batiste's assumption that discoveries are made by developing a theory and then testing it, <u>oversimplifies</u> the process.

- The study <u>manipulates / distorts</u> the findings to fit in with the initial proposition.
- In my view, we can <u>disregard / discount</u> the idea that personality has a major effect on second language acquisition.
- The small sample size should <u>alert</u> us <u>to</u> the fact that the findings may be unreliable.
- Alwald's conclusion seems to <u>conflict with</u> his earlier point that we need new legislation on drug use.
- I suggest that the Copyright Amendment Act is <u>misconceived</u> because …

Using negative adjectives and adverbs to comment on a source

- Smith's argument is <u>invalid // flawed // inconsistent // unsound // incoherent // contradictory // problematic // circular // unconvincing</u> because …
- Smith's study is <u>inconclusive // limited // questionable // unreliable // unsatisfactory</u> because the sample size is very small.
- Alwald's evidence seems <u>subjective // anecdotal // contradictory // incomplete</u>. He fails to …
- The questions in the survey used to gather the data seem somewhat <u>arbitrary // simplistic</u>.
- The report's conclusion is <u>vague</u>. It does not specify …
- Patel's model has <u>limited</u> application because it only deals with small-sized businesses.
- The novel's plot is <u>formulaic</u> and has a predictable ending.
- I will show that Peccori <u>wrongly</u> assumes that the correlation between stress and drug use is a causal one.

Using nouns to comment negatively on a source

- The argument that business and society are separate is, as I will demonstrate, a <u>fallacy</u>.
- There are both theoretical and practical <u>objections to / problems with</u> the idea of licensing parents. Firstly, …
- A <u>serious weakness in / limitation of</u> the argument is that it does not distinguish between volunteers and employees.
- A (common) <u>criticism of</u> Dawkins' position is that he overstates the role religion plays in human conflict.
- <u>The problem with</u> Kohil's argument <u>is that</u> it does not cover all possible situations.
- One <u>flaw</u> in the study is that it is <u>biased</u> towards Western cultures.
- The research team seem <u>to show a disregard for</u> proper contamination control.
- Tse <u>offers no explanation</u> as to why left-handedness might be caused by complications at birth.
- The report suffers from <u>a lack of / absence of</u> detailed analysis.
- A <u>conspicuous / noticeable omission</u> is that the analysis does not include children.
- There are several <u>digressions</u> that detract from the main argument.

- The many anecdotes are <u>a distraction</u> from the main point of the text.
- The authors <u>make no attempt to</u> present or evaluate the counterarguments.

Describing specific flaws in the logic of an argument

- The absence of women in the study means that his conclusions are an <u>overgeneralisation</u>.
- Saying that an opt-out system is good because it ensures organs are donated unless specified otherwise, is a <u>circular</u> argument.
- The minister offered the <u>non sequitur</u> that because identity theft is increasing, we should introduce identity cards.
- Ormazabal (2003) argues that there is a <u>contradiction</u> in Keynes' definition of income.
- The report concludes with the <u>tautological statement / tautology</u> that the economy will either improve or will not.
- Buchanan offered the <u>truism</u> that to achieve good public health, all sections of the community need adequate housing.
- The argument that the UK economy will be stronger if we leave the EU is <u>irrational / illogical</u> because ...

Stating that an argument is not supported by other research

- Lock's idea is <u>not supported by / not corroborated by // contradictory to // undermined by</u> other research.
- This <u>claim</u> <u>is called into question by / conflicts with / is contradicted by / is inconsistent with</u> later studies.
- <u>The problem with</u> Kohil's <u>argument is that it is not supported by (any) other evidence</u>.

Stating how research or an argument could have been better

- The report <u>would have been more</u> <u>convincing // persuasive // effective</u> if it had used more recent data.

25.2   Information to help you use these words correctly

anecdotal adj	= Information that comes from casual observation or from only one or two sources, and which is therefore not a reliable basis from which to make generalisations or draw conclusions.
arbitrary adj	= Actions or decisions that are based on unjustified, random premises and assumptions.

bias n	= The treatment of something in an unequal / partial manner. (See also section 19, page 119.)
circular adj	= A logical fallacy whereby an argument is 'empty' because the conclusion is merely a restatement of the premise(s) and so assumes as true what it is trying to prove. E.g. Wearing a helmet when cycling is advisable because it makes sense to do so.
conspicuous adj	= Clearly visible, noticeable. Often (but not always) used in a negative context. E.g. A conspicuous flaw // deficiency // absence.
contradictory adj **contradiction** n **contradict** v	= n – In argument, such that two or more statements cannot both/all be true.
detract v **detraction** n	= v – To reduce the value or worth of something or to make it seem less impressive. E.g. The diagrams detract from the main point because they are not directly related to it. *Gr* X **detracts from** Y. ≠ *Detract* and *distract* See below.
digress v **digression** n	= v – To move away from the main topic / issue. (See also section 16, page 99.)
discount v / n	= v – To disregard or leave out something because it lacks validity and/or importance. n – A deduction from the original price. * The verb is pronounced dis<u>count</u> and the noun is pronounced <u>dis</u>count.
discredit v	= (1) In academic study, to cause evidence or ideas to seem unreliable or false. (2) To damage someone's reputation in some way. *∂* To discredit an **argument** // **idea** // **theory** // **research**.

distort v **distortion** n	= v – To give a misleading or false impression, or to misrepresent. ✐ To distort (the) **facts** // **evidence** // **findings** // **results** // **truth** // **understanding** // **reality**.
distract v **distraction** n	= v – To take attention, concentration or focus away from something else. 𝒢𝓇 *Distract* must use **a direct object**. E.g. The diagrams are relevant but distract from the main point. ✗ The diagrams are relevant but distract **the reader** from the main point. ✓ ✐ X distracts Y from the **main aim** / **goal** / **purpose** / **objective**. ≠ *Distract* and *detract* These two words have different meanings – see above for *detract*.
fallacy n **fallacious** adj	= n – A commonly held idea or belief that is false. In formal logic, a fallacy is any form of incorrect reasoning that leads to an invalid argument. Examples of logical fallacies are non sequiturs (see below) and false analogies or comparisons.
flaw n **flawed** adj	= n – A defect, shortcoming or underlying weakness.
formulaic adj	= Not original or interesting because it uses a standard and much-used format.
incoherent adj	= Not logical or well structured. ✐ An incoherent **argument** // **article** // **framework** // **strategy** // **policy** // **system** // **theory**. For *coherent*, see section 24, page 159.
inconclusive adj	= Not producing a definite result or conclusion. ✐ To **be** // **remain** // **prove** inconclusive.
inconsistent adj	= (1) Unstable, changing in some way, or acting in a different way than previously. (2) Contradictory. For *consistent* see section 9, page 56.

invalid adj **invalidity** n	= adj – (1) In logic, an invalid argument is one that contains flawed reasoning, i.e. where the conclusion does not necessarily follow from the premises. A non sequitur is an example of an invalid argument. (See below.) (2) Not legally recognised. For *valid / validity* see section 24, page 162. ≠ *Invalid* and *invalid* The adjective defined here is pronounced in<u>va</u>lid. The noun, meaning someone who is frail due to illness, is pronounced <u>in</u>valid.
limited adj	= (1) Restricted or unsatisfactory in some way. See also section 8, page 51. (2) Of people, narrow minded or lacking in ability.
manipulate v	= (1) To alter or present information in a way that is purposely misleading. (2) To move, handle or control, usually by using the hands. (3) To influence and or control another person. ✲ The adjective *manipulative* is too strong and personal to use in an academic context.
misconceive v **misconception** n	= v – (1) To plan or judge something poorly or incorrectly. (2) To misunderstand. n – An incorrect belief or opinion. (See also section 18, page 113.)
non sequitur n	= A statement that does not follow logically from the one before, or a conclusion that is based on insufficient, incorrect or irrelevant reasoning. In formal logic, a non sequitur is when a conclusion does not follow from its premise(s). E.g. All bikes have wheels. This car has wheels, therefore this car is a bike.
objection n **object** v / n	= n – A reason for disagreeing with or disapproving of something. Gr To have an **objection to** something. ∂ A **chief / main / primary / principal // fundamental // formal** objection. ✲ The verb is pronounced obj<u>ect</u> and the noun is pronounced <u>ob</u>ject.
omission n **omit** v	= n – Something left out or a failure to do something.

overgeneralise v **overgeneralisation** n	= v – To make a generalisation (i.e. to apply a specific case to a wider range of situations) that is too broad to be justified. E.g. People are healthier now than they were twenty years ago. ✳ For *generalise* and *generalisation*, see section 26, page 177.
oversimplify v **oversimplification** n	= v – To explain something (usually cause and effect) so that it seems simpler than it actually is. E.g. Sugar makes you fat. ≠ *Overgeneralise* and *oversimplify* These words are often confused. As shown in the definitions here, an overgeneralisation is a statement that is incorrect because it is <u>applied</u> too broadly, not because it oversimplifies a particular situation or process. ✐ v – To **slightly // greatly** oversimplify. n – A **slight // gross** oversimplification.
questionable adj	= (1) Open to doubt or challenge regarding quality, accuracy or truth. (2) Of someone's character, not very honest or respectable.
simplistic adj	= (Much) simpler than is actually the case and therefore misleading. ✐ A simplistic **approach // argument // assumption // description // explanation // view**.
subjective adj	= Based on feelings and beliefs rather than evidence or fact. Opposite of *objective*. (See also section 19, page 117.) ✐ The newspaper article is **highly / extremely / largely // somewhat** subjective. A subjective **opinion // viewpoint // response // assessment // judgement**.
tautology n **tautological** adj	= n – A sentence or phrase that merely repeats itself. Tautologies are common in everyday language. E.g. A free gift, joined together, in close proximity.

truism n	= An obviously true and uninteresting statement that is therefore not worth making.
	≠ *Truism* and *axiom* These can be interchanged, but *axiom* can also refer to a statement that is actually useful because it establishes a basic premise or principle from which to analyse an argument. *Axiom* is often used in mathematics and philosophy and the adjective *axiomatic* is used in many disciplines. E.g. It's axiomatic to say that economic growth relies on increased production.
undermine v	= To cause something to become less confident, successful or powerful. (See section 12, page 78.)
	✎ To undermine **credibility** // **validity** // **trust** // **support** // **confidence** // **value** // **stability** // **democracy**. To undermine a/an **principle** // **argument** // **belief** // **idea** // **theory**.
vague adj vagueness n	= adj – Imprecise, indefinite or unclear.
	≠ *Vague* and *ambiguous* These words have different meanings. Something is ambiguous if it has more than one possible meaning and so may be interpreted differently in different contexts. For *ambiguous* see section 2, page 7.

25.3 Nearly but not quite right

The sentences on the left contain the types of mistakes people make when using words from this section. The correct versions are given on the right.

	Incorrect	Correct
1	The claim that diet determines cancer risk is an <u>overgeneralisation</u>.	The claim that diet determines cancer risk is an <u>oversimplification</u>.
2	The study <u>alleged</u> that mass media can be used to educate children.	The study <u>claimed / maintained / asserted / suggested</u> that mass media can be used to educate children.
3	The conclusion is <u>contradicted with</u> the data given earlier in the paper.	The conclusion is <u>contradicted by</u> the data given earlier in the paper.

	Incorrect	Correct
4	Tanen (2000) <u>established</u> that visual imprinting occurs in infancy. However, this was shown to be incorrect by later studies.	Tanen (2000) <u>claimed / maintained / contended / asserted (stated)</u> that visual imprinting occurs in infancy. However, this was shown to be incorrect by later studies.
5	Bijal <u>fails to neglect</u> the fact that in urban areas rich and poor often live in proximity.	Bijal <u>fails to consider</u> the fact that in urban areas rich and poor often live in proximity.
6	Smith's study is <u>limiting</u> because the sample size is too small.	Smith's study is <u>limited</u> because the sample size is too small.
7	The experiment was conducted according to a <u>formulaic</u> method to ensure reliability.	The experiment was conducted according to a <u>standard / prescribed</u> method to ensure reliability.
8	The arguments in Bazer's article <u>have a strong bias of</u> Eurocentric.	The arguments in Bazer's article <u>have a strong Eurocentric bias / are highly biased towards Europe</u>.
9	Hooper's theory on the HIV virus is <u>suffering from</u> lack of evidence.	Hooper's theory on the HIV virus <u>suffers from</u> lack of evidence.
10	The theory was <u>given discredit</u> when it was shown that there was no chimpanzee tissue in the remaining 1950s vaccine stocks.	The theory was <u>discredited</u> when it was shown that there was no chimpanzee tissue in the remaining 1950s vaccine stocks.

Drawing your own conclusions, stating your own position and summarising your ideas

● ● ● ● ● ●

26   Suggesting counterarguments, conceding, disagreeing, drawing your own conclusions and generating your own ideas

The final stage in synthesis is to use your evaluation to reconstruct your material in your own way, drawing your own conclusions and generating your own concepts and ideas. You can argue against a position by admitting some points (called conceding – see section 19, page 119) but disagreeing on others, or by disagreeing with all aspects of the opposing argument. In either case you must make sure that you use your analysis and evaluation of material to give valid and coherent reasons and/or evidence for your counterargument. The penultimate step in your work should be to go beyond the material, create your own concepts, draw your own conclusions (also called inferring), to generalise and to establish new ground.

Section 26 gives you vocabulary for doing all of the above. You will also need to use words and phrases from section 27 to ensure that your conclusions are not too general or extreme, and you may also want to use vocabulary from section 28 to summarise and to make recommendations.

26.1   Words in action

Suggesting counterarguments

▸ An argument against / An argument that counters / A counterargument to the theory of evolution is that life is too complex to have developed without intelligent direction.
▸ A challenge to pro-capitalism ideology is that it inevitably results in the rich getting richer and the poor getting poorer.
▸ There is good evidence for man-made causes of global warming, but an alternative theory is that the climate is regulated by atomic particles from exploded stars.

Stating contradictions

▸ The paradox of a high intake of saturated fat but low rate of heart disease, has been linked to wine consumption.

- Religious belief and scientific rationality are <u>contradictory</u> world views.

Conceding up to a point and then disagreeing

- Translators are necessary <u>but</u> can't always convey fully the author's meaning.
- <u>Although</u> translators are necessary, <u>I have shown that</u> they can't always convey the author's exact meaning.
- <u>Notwithstanding the fact that / Despite the fact that</u> translators are essential, they often can't convey …
- Translators are essential. <u>Nonetheless, / Nevertheless, / However,</u> I have shown that they cannot fully convey …
- <u>While I don't agree with</u> Dawkins that religious education is indoctrination, <u>I do think that</u> he has <u>a valid point</u> when he says …
- <u>Although I think it is going too far to say that</u> unions are redundant, <u>we should be willing to concede / accept / acknowledge that</u> …
- <u>I disagree with</u> Collins <u>on the extent to which</u> businesses should be ethical, <u>but I do agree with</u> his basic proposition.

Stating clearly that you disagree (For information on *contest, refute, reject* and *rebut* see section 23.)

- I <u>refute / contest // reject // rebut</u> Lei's <u>idea // claim // argument</u> and <u>offer the alternative suggestion that</u> …
- I <u>counter</u> Wolf's hypothesis <u>with</u> the suggestion that businesses and society are interdependent.
- <u>I don't</u> <u>agree / disagree</u> (with the view) that grammar should be taught and have shown that …
- <u>My rebuttal to</u> the argument for 'human' global warming is <u>based on the fact that</u> temperature variations are …
- <u>In my view the main</u> <u>flaw in // problem with // limitation of</u> Bernhard's hypothesis <u>is that</u> it is too restrictive. <u>I therefore / thus offer an alternative view,</u> which is that …
- I <u>would argue that the opposite is</u> <u>probably / likely to be</u> the case because …

Drawing specific conclusions (For information on *validate* and *verify*, see section 24, page 162.)

- <u>This evidence leads us to accept</u> <u>the hypothesis that / the idea that</u> intention to quit is causally linked to job satisfaction.
- The <u>inference we can make / conclusion we can draw</u> from our survey is that students would like more seminars.
- These findings <u>corroborate / confirm / are consistent with / support / verify</u> the idea that …

- This evidence <u>helps to validate</u> the waist to hip ratio and female attractiveness hypothesis.
- The events outlined <u>testify to</u> the fact that tensions between the police and the community persist.
- <u>We can infer from</u> the survey that the many women object to the images <u>on the grounds that</u> they promote exploitation.
- From our analysis <u>we can infer that</u> overall, having a job has a greater impact on happiness than the salary received.
- <u>As</u> people are on average richer but not happier than forty years ago, <u>we can conclude that</u> we should not be using …
- People are on average richer but not happier than forty years ago, which <u>implies</u> that we should not be using wealth …
- Bioinformatic data enables us <u>to deduce</u> the function sequence of individual proteins.
- <u>As</u> most species of sea snail live in saltwater, (<u>via induction / inductive reasoning</u>) new species are unlikely to be found in rivers.
- We can <u>generalise</u> from this study and suggest a link between being a victim of bullying and suicide.

Suggesting wider implications and making predictions

- The discovery of the new drug has important <u>implications</u> for all heart-related diseases.
- The introduction of the new hand-washing technique to all hospitals <u>is likely to</u> save lives.
- <u>It is possible to predict</u> future sea levels by <u>extrapolating</u> from our current data.
- The Lambda-CDM model <u>extrapolates backwards</u> in time to derive the idea of the 'big bang'.
- Global temperatures are <u>predicted to</u> rise.
- From the data the <u>projection</u> is that temperatures will rise by up to three degrees over the next twenty years.
- <u>We estimate</u> that in a fifty-year period, one tree recycles more than £60,000 worth of water.

Linking evidence to theory and giving reasons for your inference or position

- This <u>evidence shows that / suggests that</u> ex-students who stay in work for over a year have better job performance.
- <u>Evidence for</u> the concept of automatic ageism <u>can be found in</u> Purdue and Gurtman's 1988 study.
- My argument <u>is based on the findings</u> of Slovic et al. (2000). They show that …
- <u>One (possible) explanation for</u> the correlation is that young children are unable to distinguish …
- <u>My reasons for</u> suggesting a link between background and confidence <u>are</u> twofold. Firstly, …
- In coming to this conclusion, I have <u>taken into account / taken into consideration</u> the findings of all three studies.
- Porter and Kramer's <u>argument is the most persuasive / convincing because</u> …

Going further: generating your own ideas, creating new concepts and establishing new ground

▸ By looking at the issue in this way, we reach the disturbing conclusion that <u>not only</u> are children unable to distinguish games from reality, <u>but (also) that</u> violent games are actually shaping their world at a young age and thereby creating a more violent real-world view.

▸ <u>I would go even further / I would take an even stronger position</u> and suggest that crucially, the insidious nature of the ageism and the injustice individuals feel leads to a huge waste of individual, social and economic potential.

▸ <u>I would like to suggest that</u> these four artists are all <u>in fact</u> unconsciously celebrating their individual success <u>rather than just / rather than merely</u> celebrity in general.

26.2   Information to help you use these words correctly

conclusion n conclude v	= n – (1) The inference / proposition you draw from the premises. In this sense, *to conclude* is similar to *to deduce*. E.g. All of her friends are intelligent. Jos is one of her friends, **therefore Jos is intelligent.** Note that you might have several conclusions at different stages in your overall argument. (2) The end or finish of something. (See also section 28, page 188.)
contradictory adj	= Such that two or more statements cannot both/all be true.
corroborate v corroboration n	= v – To support something by giving additional data, evidence or information. Similar to *support* except that *corroborate* is usually used for concrete / empirical data rather than ideas and theories. (See also section 24.)

counter v	= To respond with an opposing argument, view or action. (See also sections 23 and 26.)
	✐ To counter **a claim** // **an argument** // **a threat** // **a criticism** // **fundamentalism** // **terrorism** // **extremism**.
	✳ To say that 'X **is counter to** Y' or 'X **runs counter to** Y' has the slightly different meaning of an action that purposely or perhaps accidentally goes against something else. E.g. Building on this site would run counter to the government's policy of maintaining green spaces.
counterargument n	= An argument that opposes another argument.
	≠ *Counterargument* and *counterclaim* In academic writing you can counter a claim someone makes. However, the noun and verb *counterclaim* are usually reserved for legal or insurance contexts. For example, after a car crash, the car owner claims for damages and the other person then counterclaims (or makes a counterclaim) for personal injury.
deduce v **deduction** n **deductive** adj	= v – To reach a conclusion through reasoning. More precisely, *to deduce* is when you use <u>general principles</u> (premises) to arrive at a <u>specific conclusion</u>. In a formal deductive argument, the premises guarantee / entail the conclusion – if the premises are valid, the conclusion must also be valid. E.g. All mammals are warm-blooded. A cow is a mammal, therefore a cow is warm-blooded. Compare with *induce / induction* below.
extrapolate v	= To extend the application of known statistical data.
generalise v **generalisation** n **generality** n	= v – To use specific data or a specific case (or several cases) to make a broader statement, i.e. one that can be said to be true in most (but not all) cases. *Generalisation* is used in a specific way in the context of formal argument and logic. Here a generalisation can be universal (e.g. 'All mammals are warm-blooded') and can therefore form a premise in deductive argument, or a generalisation can be partial (e.g. 'The London shops in our survey had high prices') and form a premise of an inductive argument. (See *inductive* below.)
	Gr n – To **make a** generalisation.

implicate v	= (1) To necessitate. In academic writing, *to implicate* is usually used in the context of formal logic. Similar to *imply* and *entail*. (2) To be shown to be involved in a crime.
implication n	= (1) A likely consequence or effect. (2) A conclusion drawn that is not stated explicitly. (3) A conclusion that follows logically from the premises. ⌕ **Important // profound // considerable // serious // wide // far-reaching // long-term** implications.
imply v	= (1) To logically necessitate a consequence or conclusion. E.g. Life implies death. (2) To enable the drawing of a conclusion. E.g. The data implies that the disease is spread via water rather than air. (3) To suggest something indirectly. E.g. His tone implied that I wasn't working hard enough. This is an informal use of *imply* not commonly used in an academic context. ≠ *Imply* and *infer* – see below. For *implicit* see section 17, page 106.
induction n **inductive** adj	= n – (1) The reasoning process we use in everyday life, whereby we take evidence from one or more <u>specific</u> cases (or what has happened so far) to draw a more <u>general conclusion / inference</u>. Importantly, the larger the evidence base used as a premise, the more sound the conclusion. Unlike in deductive reasoning (see above), a conclusion arrived at through induction cannot be proven with absolute certainty. E.g. The London shops in our survey had high prices, therefore London probably has a higher cost of living than other UK cities. E.g. Computers continue to increase in power, so by 2025 they will be much more powerful than today. (2) The process of establishing someone in a job or organisation. ✳ In most academic writing, *to induce / inductive reasoning* is something you do rather than words you use explicitly. ✳ The verb *to induct* relates only to meaning (2) of *induction*. ✳ In maths, the term 'mathematical induction' is in fact a form of deductive reasoning.

infer v **inference** n	= v – To reach a conclusion (through any type of reasoning process). ≠ *Infer* and *imply* The confusion arises when drawing conclusions (see meaning 2 of *imply* on previous page). In this context it is people that infer, and evidence and/or steps in reasoning that imply. E.g. From our data **we** can **infer** that employment is the key factor. ✓ From our data **we** can **imply** that employment is the key factor. ✗ **The data implies** that employment is the key factor. ✓
limitation n	= n – (1) A rule, restriction or situation that restricts something. (See also section 8, page 51.) (2) A failing or deficiency. E.g. The novels are important but they have limitations.
paradox n **paradoxical** adj	= n – A statement or situation where two things are apparently or actually correct but can't both be true. E.g. She is a wise fool. ≠ *Paradox* and *contradiction* *Paradox* can be used to mean a contradiction but is also more loosely used to mean a problematic or surprising situation which on closer examination can in fact be resolved (i.e. it is not a true paradox). A *contradiction* is when the elements involved are logically incompatible and the situation is therefore truly irresolvable.
predict v **predictable** adj **prediction** n	= v – To make a statement about the future, with or without basing it on evidence. adj – (1) Able to be predicted. (2) Usual, expected and therefore boring. E.g. The film's plot was predictable. ≠ *Predictable* and *predictive* These two adjectives have different meanings. *Predictive* means 'relating to predictions' or having the ability to make predictions. E.g. All mobile phones have a predictive text function. ✳ The word *scenario*, as in 'The most likely scenario is a mild recession', is too informal for academic writing. Compare with *speculation*, section 4, page 26.

project v / n	=	v – To use current evidence or information to make a statement about future developments.
	*	The verb is pronounced pro<u>ject</u> and the noun is pronounced <u>pro</u>ject.
testify v	=	(1) To give evidence as a witness in court. (2) To act as proof or evidence of something.
	Gr	X **testifies to the fact that** ... **The fact that** ... **testifies to** the significance // importance **of** Y. X **testifies that** ...
therefore adv	=	For that reason, consequently.
thus adv		(1) 'By this means'. E.g. We heated the liquid, thus creating vapour. (2) 'In this way'. E.g. Presented thus, the argument is unclear. (3) 'As a result of this / therefore'. E.g. The bid was successful and thus they were awarded the funds. (4) 'To this point / extent'. E.g. Thus far we have looked only at the national data. (See also section 20, page 132.)

26.3 Nearly but not quite right

The sentences on the left contain the types of mistakes people make when using words from this section. The correct versions are given on the right.

	Incorrect	Correct
1	Writing in English is <u>implied</u> when studying for a degree in the UK.	Writing in English is an <u>implicit</u> part of studying for a degree in the UK.
2	The data <u>infers</u> that lack of sunlight increases risk of depression.	The data <u>implies</u> that lack of sunlight increases risk of depression. or We can <u>infer</u> from the data that lack of ...
3	The company has <u>projected</u> a positive outcome despite the fact that there is no supporting data.	The company has <u>predicted</u> a positive outcome despite the fact that there is no supporting data.

	Incorrect	Correct
4	Data gathered from testing on animals cannot be <u>generalised towards</u> humans.	Data gathered from testing on animals cannot be generalised. or Data gathered from animal testing cannot be <u>applied to</u> humans.
5	One <u>insinuation</u> of this data is that the drug is not effective.	One <u>implication</u> of this data is that the drug is not effective.
6	Morley (2005) asks whether we can <u>be general about</u> current twin study data to the wider population.	Morley (2005) asks whether we can <u>generalise from</u> current twin study data to the wider population.
7	Historical patterns of migration can be <u>implied from</u> genetic data.	Historical patterns of migration can be <u>inferred from</u> genetic data. (NB 'Can be inferred' is the passive form and therefore means 'inferred by someone / us'.)
8	Evidence that globalisation is happening more slowly than commonly thought <u>is a</u> significant business <u>implication</u>.	Evidence that globalisation is happening more slowly than commonly thought <u>has</u> significant business <u>implications</u>.
9	High-definition television has higher resolution and <u>nonetheless</u> requires more bandwidth than a traditional set.	High-definition television has higher resolution and <u>so / therefore / thus</u> requires more bandwidth than a traditional set.
10	One <u>conclusion</u> Trudgill <u>makes</u> is that working-class speech patterns have more favourable connotations for men than for women.	One <u>conclusion</u> Trudgill <u>draws</u> is that working-class speech patterns have more favourable connotations for men than for women.

27 Being precise about your conclusions and expressing certainty, caution or doubt

This section gives you words and phrases for expressing your conclusions precisely. Your conclusions (also referred to as inferences) should not be too general, vague or extreme – overgeneralising is a common student error. For example, the sentence 'Globalisation is beneficial to large law firms' is an overgeneralisation, and would be better expressed as 'Globalisation is almost certainly beneficial to most large law firms.' In addition to making sure that your claims are accurate and specific, you also need to show how certain you are about them. In academic work it is rare to express total certainty, as all knowledge is open to being questioned and possibly disproved, and you will therefore usually need to express a degree of caution (also called 'being tentative').

Being specific and showing appropriate levels of caution when making claims or drawing conclusions is called 'qualification' and is a powerful way of controlling your argument and of making shifts in your direction and emphasis.

Note that when drawing your conclusions you should avoid phrases such as *Obviously ...*, *It is obvious that ...*, *We all know that ...*, *Of course, ...*, because in the context of knowledge, nothing is obvious and we don't all know things. Note also that you should use the phrases *It is clear that ...*, *Clearly, ...*, only in the context of looking at evidence. E.g. 'It is clear from the data I have presented that the model does not work.'

27.1 Words in action

Expressing degrees of certainty or caution

Being very certain about your conclusion
▸ It is <u>clear / evident / apparent</u> from the data that long-term throat damage is prevalent amongst school teachers.
▸ The findings <u>(clearly // almost certainly)</u> <u>show</u> that core personality traits are universal.
▸ The data <u>strongly / clearly</u> <u>suggest</u> a causal link between hand-washing and risk of infection.
▸ I would <u>strongly suggest that</u> globalisation is beneficial to large law firms.
▸ I have shown that there is a <u>good / strong / definite</u> <u>possibility that</u> St Paul was influenced by Mithraism.
▸ It is <u>highly probable / highly likely</u> that the key factor in safe glass design is ...
▸ The economic value of ecosystems has <u>almost certainly</u> been underestimated.

Being fairly certain about your conclusion
▸ Wilfred Owen was <u>debatably / arguably</u> the most influential poet of the First World War.

- The events <u>show / suggest</u> underlying tensions between the police and the local community.
- The events <u>seem to / appear to</u> <u>show / suggest</u> underlying tensions between the police and the local community.
- The findings <u>indicate that / show that / suggest that</u> there <u>might be / may be / could be</u> a causal relationship between …
- This <u>would seem to / would appear to</u> <u>show / indicate</u> that St Paul was influenced by Mithraism.
- It is <u>probable / likely</u> that the economic value of ecosystems has been underestimated.
- It is <u>possible</u> that globalisation is generally beneficial to large law firms.
- It is <u>conceivable</u> that within our life time, nanoparticles will be used to cure most known cancers.

Being cautious about your conclusion
- The findings <u>perhaps suggest that</u> core personality traits are universal.
- This <u>might / could</u> <u>suggest that</u> school teachers tend to suffer long-term throat damage.
- We can <u>draw only (very) tentative conclusions</u> from our data.
- There is <u>(only) a (very)</u> <u>slight / small // remote</u> <u>possibility that</u> core personality traits are universal.

Qualifying your conclusion by stating its limitations
- We need to be <u>cautious in applying</u> these findings to other situations because …
- These advantages are <u>not</u> necessarily <u>transferable</u> to all other types of organisation.
- I have looked <u>only</u> at this specific piece of legislation and so <u>cannot generalise</u> to other areas of law.
- Businesses need to be profitable. <u>Even so, / Despite this, / Nevertheless, / Nonetheless, / Notwithstanding this, / Having said that,</u> they (also) need to act within ethical boundaries.
- Businesses need to be profitable. <u>However,</u> they <u>still / also</u> need to take account of social norms.
- Further research in this area is needed. <u>Nevertheless, / Nonetheless,</u> it seems that gum disease is caused by …
- <u>Despite / In spite of / Notwithstanding the fact that</u> the drug had minor side effects, it was successful in reducing …
- <u>Despite</u> having minor side effects, the drug was successful in reducing headaches in healthy subjects.
- Dmitrieva shows that the languages share word associations for 'red', <u>albeit / although / though</u> with one or two differences.
- <u>Even though / Although</u> further research is needed, it would seem that gum disease is caused by …

Qualifying your conclusion to avoid overgeneralisation
- <u>On the whole, / By and large, / With a few exceptions, / The majority of</u> Chinese businesses …
- <u>In general / Generally, / Normally / To a large extent</u> this framework is applicable to other areas of …

- The legislation is effective <u>up to a point but</u> as I have shown, it needs revision in relation to …
- I have shown that <u>a small number of // some // many // most / the majority of</u> adverts are, <u>to some extent,</u> misleading.
- <u>Some // Many // Most</u> adverts <u>have a tendency to / tend to</u> misuse the word 'free'.

27.2 Information to help you use these words correctly

albeit conj	=	(1) 'In spite of the fact that'. Similar to *although / though / even though*. (2) 'But'.
	Gr	*Albeit* cannot introduce a whole clause. E.g. The experiment design was useful, albeit <u>it was flawed</u>. ✗ The experiment design was useful, albeit flawed. ✓
although conj **even though** conj **though** conj	=	(1) 'In spite of the fact that'. (2) 'But'. *Although, though* and *even though* have similar meanings – they all qualify a statement or make it seem unexpected or surprising. *Although* is more common than *though*. *Even though* is the most informal and indicates a stronger degree of surprise.
	Gr	*Although* and *though* can be used with only an **adjective** but *even though* must always introduce <u>a whole clause</u>. E.g. The experiment design was useful although / though **flawed**. ✓ The experiment design was useful even though **flawed**. ✗ The experiment design was useful even though <u>it was flawed</u>. ✓
apparent adj **apparently** adv	=	adj – (1) Clear and obvious. E.g. It is apparent from the size of the protest that people are concerned about the issue. (2) Seeming to be or to exist, when in fact it is not (or might not be) real or correct. E.g. Sears and Burrows compared responses between asthmatic and apparently healthy children.
	✱	The use of *apparently* to mean 'according to rumour or gossip' (e.g. Apparently, they still don't know the real cause of the accident) is too informal for academic study.

arguable adj **arguably** adv	= adj – Open to argument or disagreement. Similar to *debatable*. adv – It may be challenged or disagreed with. Similar to *debatably*. (See also section 4, page 22.)
conceivable adj **conceivably** adv	= adj – (1) Within the realms of possibility and capable of being imagined. (2) Possible but unlikely.
debatable adj **debatably** adv	= adj – Open to argument or disagreement. Similar to *arguable*. adv – It may be argued or disagreed with. Similar to *arguably*. (See also section 1, page 3.)
	≠ *Debatable* and *doubtful* The use of *debatable* to mean *doubtful* is informal, so in academic writing only use *debatable* to mean 'open to argument'. E.g. It is debatable whether the experiment can be repeated successfully. ✗ It is doubtful / uncertain whether the experiment can be repeated successfully. ✓ I will outline the debatable issues surrounding the theory of evolution. ✓
evident adj **evidently** adv	= adj – Clear / obvious. Similar to meaning (1) of *apparent*.
nevertheless adv **nonetheless** adv	= 'Despite this fact' / 'even so'.
	Gr When *nevertheless* / *nonetheless* start a new clause, they should also start a new sentence. E.g. Gum disease is common, nevertheless/nonetheless, it is caused by … ✗ Gum disease is common. Nevertheless/Nonetheless, it is caused by … ✓
notwithstanding prep / conj	= prep – 'In spite of'. E.g. We conducted the experiment, notwithstanding the lack of equipment.
probable adj	= Likely to happen.
	∂ **Highly** probable. A probable **outcome** // **effect** // **consequence** // **impact** // **cost** // **loss**.
tentative adj	= Cautious, hesitant.
	∂ To **draw a** tentative **conclusion**. To **make a** tentative **suggestion** // **inference**.

27.3 Nearly but not quite right

The sentences on the left contain the types of mistakes people make when using words from this section. The correct versions are given on the right.

	Incorrect	Correct
1	Rural areas have higher levels of poverty than cities.	*Many / Most / Some rural areas have higher levels of poverty than cities. *Or other similar qualifying phrase.
2	Apparently, the data contains some minor errors.	It is apparent that the data contains some minor errors. or The data clearly contains some minor errors.
3	I am uncertain as to whether the experiment shows that this species of starfish still inhabits intertidal zones.	The experiment *perhaps suggests that this species of starfish still inhabits intertidal zones. (*Or other similar qualifying phrase.)
4	Obviously, a translation can never be as good as the original version.	I have demonstrated that / I have shown that a translation is *rarely as good as the original version. (*Or other similar qualifying phrase.)
5	It's not even remotely possible that there is a causal link.	A causal link is highly unlikely / is highly improbable.
6	String theory is the most exciting current area of mathematical physics.	String theory is arguably the most exciting current area of mathematical physics. or In my view, string theory is the most exciting current area of mathematical physics.
7	From the research it is clear-cut that discrimination has decreased.	From the research it is clear that discrimination has decreased.
8	It is indeterminate whether creating habitat corridors can compensate for overall habitat loss.	It is unclear whether creating habitat corridors can compensate for overall habitat loss.

	Incorrect	Correct
9	People are more likely to cooperate if they think there is a <u>high possibility</u> of meeting the person again.	People are more likely to cooperate if they think there is a <u>good / strong possibility</u> of meeting the person again.
10	The <u>tendency of comparing</u> oneself to others is a much more complex process than previously thought.	The <u>tendency to compare</u> oneself to others is a much more complex process than previously thought.

28 Summarising, restating your ideas, and suggesting ability, potential, and future actions

The word *conclusion* has two different meanings in academic work. One meaning is inferring from your evidence, i.e. to draw conclusions, and vocabulary for this is covered in sections 26 and 27. The other meaning of *conclusion* is the last (concluding) part of a piece of writing or speech that contains a summary of the main points and conclusions reached, followed by final comments about recommendations, future research and further questions. Section 28 gives you words and phrases for this concluding part of your assignment.

Note that you will probably need to make intermediate summaries and conclusions at various stages throughout your piece of work – your final conclusion should summarise these 'mini conclusions' and draw them together with some overarching statements.

Note that the content of your conclusion is more important than using phrases such as *To summarise ...*, *In summary...*, *To conclude ...* or *In conclusion ...* and that you can write an excellent conclusion without them. Also note that you should not use informal phrases such as *In a nutshell, ...*, *Basically, ...* or *At the end of the day, ...* as they do not have any meaningful content.

28.1 Words in action

Initial summary remarks

▸ <u>In this essay I have addressed</u> the issue of whether stem cell research is ethical.
▸ <u>This essay has evaluated</u> the arguments for and against euthanasia, using specific examples and cases.
▸ <u>I have argued that</u> ageism can be viewed as more disabling than aging because ...
▸ <u>This report has assessed</u> the advantages of globalisation for law firms in the UK.
▸ <u>This report has clarified</u> the main legal issues surrounding data mining and has <u>demonstrated</u> how ...
▸ <u>I have given an account of</u> the main way in which children learn the word meanings, <u>namely / that is,</u> latent semantic analysis.
▸ <u>We have highlighted</u> five main legal and ethical issues faced by professional nurses.
▸ The <u>purpose / aim of this essay has been to</u> examine the term 'democracy'. I have done this via ...

Summarising, restating and emphasising your main point

Summarising your conclusions

▸ The evidence has caused me to <u>modify / alter / shift // change my original position (slightly)</u> because ...
▸ <u>To summarise, a key</u> motivating <u>factor</u> in human evolution appears to be innate curiosity.
▸ <u>As stated above, our research has</u> <u>shown that // found that</u> teaching standards in junior schools have ...

- The analysis <u>has exposed / has revealed / has identified</u> a major loophole in the current legislation.
- <u>The above</u> evaluation // analysis <u>confirms / verifies / supports</u> <u>the view that</u> mobile phones do not carry health risks.
- <u>I have justified</u> my position / my initial proposition / my claim <u>by</u> present<u>ing</u> specific, real-life examples of …
- <u>Our study has contributed to</u> the debate on food labelling <u>in that it</u> has provided data on how …

Restating and emphasising your conclusions
- The data suggests that the father has a relatively minor role <u>or rather,</u> that the mother has the primary impact on …
- The data suggests that the father has a relatively minor role. <u>In other words, / Put another way, / To be more precise,</u> the mother has the primary impact on …
- <u>What I am saying is that / What I want to stress is that</u> the underlying issue for all addicts is one of feeling powerless.
- I wish to <u>emphasise / stress / underline</u> the need for the police to continue recording the ethnicity of …
- Waist to hip ratio does seem to be a factor in female attractiveness. <u>Indeed, / In fact,</u> I would suggest that it is a key indicator.
- <u>It is worth noting / It should be noted / It is worth remembering / It is important to remember / It is important to bear in mind / We</u> <u>should bear in mind</u> that all living languages are evolving continuously.
- The <u>fundamental / essential / primary</u> <u>point is that</u> control systems need to take into account how a building is used.
- <u>In essence,</u> economics is the study of how individuals, societies and nations behave in response to material constraints.
- <u>Of paramount importance is</u> // <u>Of particular importance is / Of particular significance is</u> the feeling of powerlessness experienced by …
- <u>Most importantly,</u> many first-time mothers feel powerless in the hospital environment.

Stating ability and potential (See also section 26 for vocabulary to discuss wider implications.)
- The future <u>prospects</u> of UK law firms look positive, <u>provided</u> they address the above issues.
- An <u>ability</u> to adapt quickly to new situations will be <u>paramount</u> to companies in this sector.
- The analysis suggests that most people are <u>capable of</u> making positive lifestyle choices.
- Feiner suggests that Augmented Reality (AR) <u>has the potential to</u> radically change our lives.
- The report presents a <u>viable</u> alternative to the current system. It shows that …

Referring to your findings and giving recommendations for future research

▸ These findings will <u>help to improve // help to refine</u> the design of factory buildings and the way in which they <u>use / utilise</u> solar panels.

▸ <u>These findings can be used to</u> help re-orientate teacher training programmes.

▸ The findings <u>accentuate</u> the need for new legislation to protect online privacy.

▸ Our analysis demonstrates that hospitals <u>should implement // should enforce // should maintain</u> a strict hand-washing regime.

▸ From our analysis it seems clear that <u>the priority should be</u> for universities <u>to reassess / to re-examine</u> how they …

▸ <u>My analysis suggests that</u> the responsibility for global warming <u>ultimately</u> lies with the developed economies.

▸ <u>More research // Further analysis</u> on bullying in schools <u>needs to be conducted in order to</u> <u>enhance / add to / further</u> our understanding of this issue.

▸ We hope that further large-scale surveys <u>are feasible / are practicable / will be possible</u>.

▸ <u>A question for future research is</u> whether a way can be found <u>to reconcile</u> the different transfer methods.

Giving recommendations for specific future action

▸ <u>The key recommendation of this report is that</u> ongoing staff training <u>is needed to tackle</u> workplace discrimination.

▸ We <u>advocate / propose</u> shorter custodial sentences for this group of offenders.

▸ <u>In order to</u> <u>achieve / attain // ensure</u> sustainable growth, the company <u>needs to</u> limit new investment.

▸ <u>The measures</u> listed above <u>need to be taken / need to be adopted</u> in order to <u>resolve the</u> <u>problem of / issue of</u> …

▸ I suggest that <u>in order to</u> <u>adapt / adjust to</u> the new market forces, organisations <u>need to</u> continually <u>monitor</u> …

▸ Firms should be more active <u>in pre-empting</u> the market by buying suitable …

▸ Companies <u>need</u> a more <u>pragmatic // effective approach</u> to collaborations <u>in order to fully exploit</u> technological opportunities.

▸ <u>If we are to harness the potential of</u> this technology fully, <u>we need</u> an increase in government funding of at least two per cent.

▸ A possibly more <u>sustainable alternative to</u> traditional forms of fracking <u>is</u> the use of aviation hydrovibrators.

Giving more general recommendations

▸ <u>The long-term aim should be to</u> empower patients <u>so that</u> they can take fuller responsibility for their health.

▸ Local councils <u>should not overestimate // should not underestimate</u> the impact that their planning policies will have on …

▸ The <u>ultimate goal should be to</u> determine the primary cause of the erosion.

▸ Apprenticeship schemes <u>will help to equip</u> young people with important job and life skills.

▸ <u>Increased collaboration</u> between countries <u>is likely to help reduce</u> theft of telecommunications services.

▸ Transparent guidelines <u>will help to restore</u> public trust in the media.

28.2　Information to help you use these words correctly

accentuate v	= To emphasise and/or make more noticeable.
advocate v	= To support or propose something.
attain v	= To reach a goal, or to succeed in doing something.
capable adj **capability** n	= n – Ability to do something (but without necessarily doing it). *Gr* Capable **of** doing X. ≠ *Capability, ability, capacity* and *facility* *Capability / capable* and *ability / able* can sometimes be interchanged, but there is a difference between the two sets of words. *Capability / capable* are often used in the context of possibility to refer to things that might or might not be done. E.g. Zimbardo believes that we are all capable of committing evil acts. *Ability / able* are used in the context of real-world action (often skills) for things that are actually done or will be done. E.g. The new machine gives us the ability to deal with large items and improve our productivity. *Capacity* refers to the maximum physical volume / amount / extent to which something can be containedor done. E.g. He has a great capacity for hard work. In addition to this meaning, *capacity to do* X is interchangeable with *capable of doing* X.

	Facility usually refers to a building or service. E.g. The university has state of the art sports facilities. However, *facility* can also be used to mean 'natural talent' (e.g. I have a facility for learning languages) and the verb *to facilitate* means *to help*. (See section 12, page 77.)
collaborate v	= To work with someone else or others towards a common goal. ℮ **Active / close / productive / successful** collaboration. To **encourage / facilitate / foster / promote / support** collaboration.
effective adj **effectiveness** n	= adj – Having the desired outcome / effect. ≠ *Effective* and *efficient* *Efficient* means making the best possible use of time, effort, energy, money etc. Something can therefore be effective (successful) but not use resources well and so be inefficient. Something may also use resources well (be efficient) but ultimately fail to have the desired result and so be ineffective. (For *effect*, see section 20, page 130.)
essence n	= The essential part or meaning of something. ℮ **In** essence, X is … X is, **in** essence …
exploit v	= v – To make the best use of something for oneself (sometimes unfairly). ℮ To exploit a **situation // opportunity // weakness // fear // gap // loophole // advantage // crisis**.
feasible adj **feasibility** n	= adj – Possible. Likely to be successful and not difficult to do.
implement v **implementation** n	= v – To put into action / use. ℮ To implement an/a **idea // plan // policy // strategy // proposal // scheme**. To implement **guidelines // recommendations // measures // reforms // change**. To **agree // attempt / try // force // refuse // fail** to implement.
maintain v	= (1) To claim something or to defend a proposition. (See sections 24 and 25.) (2) To keep or look after. ℮ (3) To maintain **control // balance // stability // status**.

paramount adj	= More important than anything else.
	Gr X **is** paramount. **It is** paramount **that** …
practical adj / n	= adj – Related to real-world actions that are also effective and useful.
	✐ Practical **issue // problem // solution // advice // suggestion // support // skill // knowledge // support**.
	≠ *Practical* and *practicable* *Practicable* means possible / feasible.
pragmatic adj **pragmatism** n	= adj – (1) Related to real-world reasoning and results rather than theory. (See also section 18, page 114.) (2) Done in order to achieve practical results, or action taken for practical reasons.
pre-empt v	= To take action before someone else or in anticipation of a future event.
reconcile v	= To make different things agree, or to allow things to exist together.
(re)orientate v	= To (re)position in a particular direction or towards something.
sustain v **sustainability** n	= v – To provide the conditions for existence or for continued support.
	✐ To sustain X **financially // economically // on a long-term basis // indefinitely**. To sustain **employment // growth // funding // interest // the population**.
tackle v	= To deal with a problem in an organised manner.
	✐ To tackle a **problem // challenge // issue // question**.
utilise v	= To use successfully / with the desired result, usually in a practical, physical context.
	≠ *Utilise* and *use* *Use* is much more common than *utilise* and is interchangeable with *utilise*. *Utilise* can sound a bit too formal and is only used in contexts where the use is practical and effective.

viable adj	=	Realistically possible.

	✐	**Economically // commercially // financially // politically** viable. A viable **alternative // plan // option // method // strategy // approach // solution // proposition**. To **consider / deem** something viable.

28.3   Nearly but not quite right

The sentences on the left contain the types of mistakes people make when using words from this section. The correct versions are given on the right.

	Incorrect	Correct
1	This essay has demonstrated that discrimination in the workplace can be <u>reconciled</u>.	This essay has demonstrated that discrimination in the workplace can be <u>reduced // eliminated</u>.
2	There is <u>doubt on</u> the harmful physical effects of mobile phones.	There is <u>doubt about</u> the harmful physical effects of mobile phones.
3	We need to be cautious <u>to apply</u> the findings to a wider context.	We need to be cautious <u>in how we apply / in applying</u> the findings to a wider context.
4	Improved safety procedures will need a significant amount of time and effort <u>placed to it</u>.	Improved safety procedures will need a significant amount of time and effort.
5	<u>There has to be</u> a solution to the problem of drug use among young people.	<u>We need to continue working towards</u> a solution to the problem of drug use among young people.
6	The <u>case</u> of growing obesity in the UK will only be <u>solved</u> if the lobbying power of food manufactures is curtailed.	The <u>issue / problem</u> of growing obesity in the UK will only be <u>resolved</u> if the lobbying power of food manufactures is curtailed.
7	The bank should <u>bear the consequences</u> of its <u>wrong</u> financial transactions.	The bank should <u>take responsibility for / be accountable for</u> the <u>consequences of / effects of</u> its (illegal // immoral) financial transactions.
8	Our recommendation is that small businesses should <u>corroborate</u> more with local councils.	Our recommendation is that small businesses should <u>collaborate</u> more with local councils.

	Incorrect	Correct
9	I have <u>summarised at the end that</u> translations can not only be as good as the original but can even be an improvement.	In summary, <u>my key point is</u> that translations can not only be as good as the original but can even be an improvement.
10	<u>At the end of the day,</u> there is clear evidence that if you speak two or more languages it is easier to learn further languages.	There is clear evidence that if you speak two or more languages it is easier to learn further languages.

Appendix

Latin abbreviations and phrases

Points to note:

Abbreviations
- The abbreviation *etc.* is too 'lazy' and meaningless for academic writing and so should not be used. The abbreviations *e.g.* and *i.e.* are too informal to use in your assignments unless used within round brackets (called parentheses).
- Don't confuse *e.g.* and *i.e.* – they have different meanings.
- If you do use an abbreviation, make sure you use full stops and spacing correctly (see chart below).

- Common Latin abbreviations do not use italics (except for *sic*) as they are now part of the English language. They are put in italics in the chart below only when they are being discussed explicitly, to differentiate them from the rest of the text.
- Latin abbreviations are not capitalised except for the abbreviation *NB*.

Phrases
- Latin phrases are appropriate to use in your writing but are much less common than they used to be, and you shouldn't use them just to make your writing look academic.
- Common Latin phrases do not use italics as they are now part of the English language. They are put in italics in the chart below only when they are being discussed explicitly, to differentiate them from the rest of the text.
- Latin phrases are not capitalised, except for the abbreviation *NB*.

Common Latin abbreviations and phrases

Abbreviation	Full form (Not normally used in writing.)	Modern meaning	Points to note
e.g.	exempli gratia	for example, such as	In your assignment use *e.g.* only inside parentheses: E.g. Some infectious diseases (e.g. cholera and typhoid) have yet to be eradicated completely. Otherwise, use *for example* E.g. Some infectious diseases, for example cholera and typhoid, have yet to be eradicated completely. *E.g.* has a full stop after each letter because each one is an abbreviation of a word.
i.e.	id est	namely, that is to say	If you use *i.e.* (or *that is* or *namely*) you must list **all** the members of the set, not just one or two examples. In your assignment use *i.e.* only inside parentheses: E.g. Only one infectious disease (i.e. smallpox) has a completely effective vaccine. It's better to use *namely* or *that is to say.* E.g. Only one infectious disease, namely smallpox, has a completely effective vaccine. *i.e.* has a full stop after each letter because each one is an abbreviation of a word.
etc.	et cetera	and so on, and others	You should not use *etc.* in formal writing. Ending a sentence with *etc.* (or in fact with *and so on* or *and so forth*) is too lazy and vague for academic work. E.g. Having a healthy lifestyle means eating well etc. ✗ Instead, finish your sentence with as much precision as possible. E.g. Having a healthy lifestyle means eating well, exercising regularly and generally maintaining a healthy body and mind. ✓ There are no gaps in *etc.* and only one full stop at the end, because only the *c* is an abbreviation.

Abbreviation	Full form (Not normally used in writing.)	Modern meaning	Points to note
ca. c. circ. cca.	circa	(of time) approximately, around, between these dates	You can use any of the abbreviations or the complete word *circa* in formal writing. Note that the full form *circa* does not have a full stop as it is not an abbreviation. E.g. Antique paste *jewellery* was made *circa* 1700–1865.
viz.	videlicet	namely, that is to say	Similar meaning and use to *i.e.* but much less common and emphasises the clarification of the point being made. As with *i.e.*, if you must use *viz.* you must list all the members of the set, not just one or two examples. E.g. She was given a long prison sentence, viz., 25 years.

Abbreviations or words used when giving references and in endnotes, footnotes or bibliographies

Abbreviation	Full form (Not normally used in writing.)	Modern meaning	Points to note
et al.	et alii	and other authors	Use *et al.* to give an endnote or footnote reference that has more than two or three authors, depending on referencing style. Some referencing styles also allow the use of *et al.* within the body of a text (check your referencing guide). E.g. Lakmis and Knowles et al. (2006) state that … There is a space after *et* and a full stop after *al.* (not after *et* because it is not an abbreviation).

Abbreviation	Full form (Not normally used in writing.)	Modern meaning	Points to note
cf.	confer	compare with	Used in footnotes or with parentheses to draw the reader's attention to a work that contrasts in some way to the one just mentioned. 6. Liddle (2000); cf. Ford (1987).
NB N.b n.b.	nota bene	take note	Used in notes and footnotes – do not use in the main body of your writing. *N.B.* is capitalised and has a full stop after each letter.
ibid.	ibidem	the same work as the previous one	*Ibid.* is not normally used in the main body of a text but in footnotes to avoid having to name the same reference repeatedly. 1. Lupton 1985, pp. 20–30. 2. Ibid., p. 51. 3. Ibid. Note that: you can use *ibid.* with different page numbers; you cannot use *ibid.* to refer to a previous work if there is a reference to a different work in between; *ibid.* starts with a capital letter if it starts a sentence; there is a full stop after *ibid.* because it is an abbreviation.
infra	infra	see below	Not commonly used. Use *see below* instead. No full stops because it is not an abbreviation.
supra	supra	see above	Not commonly used. Use *see above* instead. No full stops because is not an abbreviation.
sic	sic	this error is in the original text	Used when using a quotation that has an error, to make clear to the reader that the mistake is not yours but is contained in the original text. E.g. The report stated that '93% of students have there [*sic*] work returned within three weeks.' *sic* uses italics and square brackets but does not have a full stop as it is not an abbreviation.

Abbreviation	Full form (Not normally used in writing.)	Modern meaning	Points to note

loc. cit.	loco citato	in the same place (page and work) as the previous reference	Used in endnotes and footnotes to avoid repeating the same reference. *Loc. cit.* is used when both the work and page number is the same as in the previous reference.
			    1. Lupton 1985, pp. 20–30.
			    2. Op. cit., p. 51.
			    3. Loc. cit.
			 Ibid. is now usually used rather than *loc. cit.*

op. cit.	opera citato	in the same work as the previous reference	Used in endnotes and footnotes to avoid repeating the same reference. *Op. cit.* is used when the work is the same as in the preceding reference but has different page numbers.
			    1. Lupton 1985, pp. 20–30.
			    2. Op. cit., p. 51.
			    3. Loc. cit.
			 Ibid. is now usually used rather than *op. cit.*

passim	passim	found in several or many places in the named work	Used with a reference to indicate that the idea occurs in many places throughout the source. Use *passim* with great caution and only if there really are too many page numbers to reference. *Passim* is not an abbreviation and so has no full stop.

Phrases used in the body of a piece of writing (these are not abbreviations and so do not use full stops)

a posteriori	Knowledge or conclusion obtained by experience and observation (inductive reasoning).
a priori	Knowledge or conclusion obtained purely through abstract reasoning or logic (deductive reasoning).
ab initio	Starting from scratch, from the beginning, at beginner's level.
ad hoc	Created or done for a specific, one-off reason or occasion. Not planned or based on any particular principle.
ad infinitum	Without end, endlessly.
bona fide	Done in good faith, genuine.
de facto	Actually existing or happening, even if not legally recognised / sanctioned.
de jure	Existing by legal right.
ex post facto	After the fact or event.
in situ	In the original or natural position.
in toto	In its entirety, altogether.
inter alia	Among other things.
prima facie	A self-evident truth or fact. At first glance or on the surface.
pro rata	Proportional to.
per se	In or of itself, intrinsically. (See section 3, page 17.)
sine qua non	An essential condition.
quid pro quo	To give in return, reciprocity.
status quo	The standard or normal situation or status.

A brief explanation of word class

Note that some words can belong to more than one word class depending on how they are used. *Debate* used as a verb. E.g. The government will debate the motion next week.
Debate used as a noun. E.g. There has been a great deal of debate on the ethics of cloning.

Noun (n)

A noun is a thing, place or person. Proper nouns are names of specific people or places, and abstract nouns (for example, *happiness* and *economics*) are nouns that you can't actually see or touch. Some nouns are uncountable / mass nouns (for example, *evidence*, *information* and *importance*) and are used in the singular form only. To talk about an uncountable noun in the plural you need to add another noun that indicates the plural aspect.

uncountable noun	incorrect use ✗	examples of correct use ✓
evidence	... the evidences are ...	... the different types of evidence are ...
information	... several informations ...	... several pieces of information ...
importance	... several importances ...	... several important aspects ...

Verb (v)

A verb is an action, event or state. The verbs *be*, *do* and *have* can be used on their own as a main verb or as a supporting (auxiliary) verb together with a main verb. As supporting verbs, *be*, *do* and *have* indicate either time, a negative or a question.

be, do, have as a **main verb**	**be, do, have** as a supporting/auxiliary verb + *main verb*
I **am** happy. I **was** happy. I **do** the same thing every day. I **have** a car.	I **am** *studying* journalism **Do** you **want** the job? I **don't** *want* the job. I **haven't** *seen* the film.

The verbs *will, shall, can, could, may, might, must, should, ought to* and *would* (and the phrases *to be able to, to need to* and *to have to*) are always used as supporting verbs with a second main verb to express possibility, request, necessity, certainty or caution. These verbs are called modal or modal auxiliary verbs. They are called modal verbs because they indicate the 'mood' of the main verb.

Modal verb + *main verb*
We **should** *consider* all aspects of the issue. The data suggest that there **might** *be* a link.

Adjective (adj)
Adjectives describe a characteristic or quality of a noun. E.g. It is an **arguable** issue.
Some adjectives have a comparative and a superlative form. E.g. Large, larger, largest.

Adverb (adv)
Adverbs give more information about a verb, adjective or another adverb, as in the following examples.
An **adverb** describing a *verb*. E.g. The economy *improved* **slowly**.
An **adverb** describing an *adjective*. E.g. It is **arguably** an *important* issue.
An **adverb** describing another **adverb**. E.g. We added the liquid **very carefully**.

Preposition (prep)
Prepositions describe the time or space relationship between things.
Examples of prepositions are *in, at, on, of, to, with, over, under, between, through, during, before, after*. Note that the word *to* is usually used as a preposition (e.g. 'She went to the conference') but is also used to indicate the infinitive of a verb (e.g. *to discuss*) and has one use as an adverb ('She pulled the window to before going to sleep').

Conjunction (conj)
Conjunctions link phrases or clauses within a sentence or link separate sentences, showing the logical relationship between them. Examples of conjunctions are *and, in addition, also, moreover, but, either … or, both … and, not only … but also, however, nevertheless, despite, after, before, since, while, until*. Some words such as *after, before, as, since* and *until* can also be used as prepositions.

Pronoun (pron)
Pronouns replace full nouns. A pronoun usually refers to a full noun or noun phrase that precedes it.
The subject pronouns are *I, you, he, she, it, we* and *they*.
E.g. *The diagrams* in the text distract the reader from the main argument and **they** also overcomplicate the issue.
The object pronouns are *me, you, him, her, it, us* and *them*.
E.g. Our results indicate that *job satisfaction* is less important for new employees. **It** also seems to be less important for part-time employees.
The possessive pronouns are *mine, yours, his, hers, its, ours, theirs* and *whose*. E.g. *This book* is **mine**.
The reflexive pronouns are *myself, yourself, himself, herself, itself, oneself, ourselves, yourselves* and *themselves*.
E.g. Virginian Woolf thought of **herself** as a writer from an early age.

Note that pronouns are useful for linking ideas and sentences and for avoiding repetition. However, a common error is to use pronouns where it is unclear what they refer to because the preceding clause or sentence has more than one subject or object.

E.g. Smith disagrees with Wolf on the issue of business ethics. **He** states that …

This sentence is unclear because we are not sure whether *he* refers to Smith or to Wolf. A clearer sentence would be:

Smith disagrees with Wolf on the issue of business ethics. Wolf states that …

Determiner (det)

Determiners give more information about a noun. There are four types of determiners:

• **Articles** *A* and *the*

• **Demonstratives** *This, these, that* and *those*
The demonstratives *this* and *these* can be used in a similar way to pronouns but unlike pronouns you can use both a demonstrative and a noun together to make your meaning more clear.

E.g. At the conference representatives from the six countries had a heated debate about how to balance economic development with sustainable use of resources. **This** is causing increasing controversy across the globe.

In this sentence it is unclear whether *this* refers to the conference, to the heated debate, or to the issue of balancing development and use of resources. A clearer sentence would be:

E.g. At the conference representatives from the six countries had a heated debate about how to balance economic development with sustainable use of resources. **This issue** is causing increasing controversy across the globe.

• **Possessive determiners** (also called possessive adjectives)
My, your, his, her, its, our and *their*. These are not pronouns because they do not replace a noun but are used with one.
E.g. This is her thesis.

• **Quantifiers**
These are words such as *all, some, each, every, few, several, many* and *most*.

Index: section headings and subheadings

Index: words and phrases

(Page numbers for words or phrases show where they are used in a sentence, and page numbers in bold indicate where the definition of a word is given.)

contrary 152, to 55
contrast 134, 136
contribute 189,
    to 126
contribution to 158
controversial 2
controversy 2, **3**
converge 150, **153**
convergence 135, **138**
converse 127, **128**
convey 105, **105**, 126,
    128
convincing 158, 166,
    176
correct 158
correlation 127, **128**
correspond 134, **138**
corresponding 127,
    129
corroborate 158, **160**,
    175, **176**
counter 152, **153**, 173,
    177
counteract 80, **81**
counterargument 173,
    177
counterpart 134, **138**
cover 157, 164
created by 126
credible 158, **160**
credit, fail to 152
criterion 13, **15**
critical 21, **23**, 96, **99**
criticise **23**, 152
critique 23
crucial 1, **3**, 96

cumulative 68
current 41, **44**
currently 44
curtail 75, **76**

damaging 97
data 55, **57**
de facto **201**
de jure **201**
dearth 90, **92**
debatably 21, **23**, 182,
    184
debate 1, **3**
decelerate 67
decline 67
deconstruct 144, **146**
decrease 67
deduce 175, **177**
deduction **177**
deficiency 91, **92**
degree of 60, **62**
demonstrate 157, 188
denote 105, **105**
dense 85, **86**
deny 80
dependent 127, **129**
depict 105, **106**
depletion 91, **92**
deprived 91, **92**
derived from 126, **129**
descriptive 20, **23**
despite 174, this 183
detect 55, **57**
deter 75, **76**, 80, **81**
deteriorate 75, **76**
determine 127, **129**

demonstratives **204**
detract 75, 97,
    from 164, **167**
detrimental 97, **99**
deviate 85
dichotomy 13, 135,
    138
differ 135
difference 135
different 151
differentiate 12, 135,
    138
digress 97, **99**, 165,
    167
dimension 61, **62**
diminish 67, **70**
disadvantage 90, **92**
disadvantaged 91, **92**
disagree 174,
    with 152
disagreement 117
discern 55, 57, 135
discord 117, **119**
discount 165, **167**
discredit 164, **167**
discrepancy 55, **57**
discrete 13, 135, **139**,
    144, **146**, 151
discriminate 117, **120**
discuss 20, **24**
disinterested 117, **120**
disparate 137, **139**,
    145, **146**
disparity 135, **139**
dispel 80, **81**
dispersed 85, **86**

disprove 164
disregard 165
disrupt 75
disseminate 104, **106**
dissimilar 135
dissociate 144, **146**
distinct 13, 135, **139**,
    144, **146**, 151
distinction 13, 135,
    139
distinguish 135, **140**
distinguished 12
distort 165, **168**
distorted 117
distract from 164
distraction 165, **168**
diverge 136, **140**, 151,
    153
diverse 137, 151
divert 97, **99**
dogma 111, **112**
domain 11, **15**
dominant 96, **99**
downward 68
dramatic 67
drawback 90
due to 126, **130**
duration 42
dynamic 127, **130**

ease 75
effect 125, **130**
effective 49, **51**, 166,
    190, **192**
e.g. **197**
elaborate on 20, **24**

Notes

Notes

Notes